THE CHOMSKY-FOUCAULT DEBATE

The Chomsky-Foucault Debate

ON HUMAN NATURE

Noam Chomsky and Michel Foucault

THE NEW PRESS

NEW YORK
LONDON

Compilation © 2006 by The New Press
Foreword © 2006 by John Rajchman

"Human Nature: Justice vs. Power" originally appeared in *Reflexive Water:
The Basic Concerns of Mankind*, published by Souvenir Press in 1974.
Reprinted by permission of Souvenir Press Ltd.

"Politics" and "A Philosophy of Language" appear as Chapters 1 and 3,
respectively, in Part I of *On Language*, published by The New Press in 1998.

"Truth and Power," "*Omnes et Singulatim*," and "Confronting Governments"
appear in *Power: Essential Works of Foucault, 1954–1984*,
published by The New Press in 2001.

Permission to reprint "*Omnes et Singulatim*" courtesy of the University of
Utah Press and the Trustees of the Tanner Lectures on Human Values.

Requests for permission to reproduce selections from this book
should be mailed to: Permissions Department, The New Press,
38 Greene Street, New York, NY 10013.

Published in the United States by The New Press, New York, 2006
Distributed by W. W. Norton & Company, Inc., New York

ISBN-13 978-1-59558-134-1 (pbk)
ISBN-10 1-59558-134-0 (pbk)
CIP data available

The New Press was established in 1990 as a not-for-profit alternative
to the large, commercial publishing houses currently dominating
the book publishing industry. The New Press operates in the
public interest rather than for private gain, and is committed to publishing,
in innovative ways, works of educational, cultural, and community
value that are often deemed insufficiently profitable.

www.thenewpress.com

Composition by dix!
This book was set in Bell MT Regular

Printed in the United States of America

2   4   6   8   10   9   7   5   3

Contents

Foreword

The initial exchange took place in Holland in November of 1971. Noam Chomsky spoke in English, Michel Foucault in French, with the results broadcast on Dutch television. It was part of a series of debates in which the Dutch thinker Fons Elders invited pairs of philosophers from different, sometimes opposing, strains in twentieth-century thought to confront one another on television.[1] Yet neither Chomsky nor Foucault was in fact a philosopher in the narrow academic sense; each had developed a highly original approach to the study of language and had subsequently gone on to assume the role of a political or public intellectual.

1971 is not a bad date for the transition from language-analysis to politics in their work. The events of 1968 were still fresh, providing a new climate of debate, introducing new divisions, and new actors, on an international (or, as it is now said, "transnational") scale, beyond any particular political or economic regime—in Prague as well as Berkeley, Paris, Mexico City, and Asia. Onto the intellectual divisions in the Elders debates, another dimension was thus superimposed. How should intellectuals affected by these events in different places talk with one another? What were the models for the new kinds of questions and new ways of posing them emerging from the political movements in so many places? Were older, more or less Marxist models sufficient, or should one draw from other Enlightenment traditions, or from the particular transformations taking place—for example, civil disobedience or participatory democracy? Moving back and forth in two languages for a Dutch television audience at this peculiar moment, passing from questions of language and creativity to power and politics, the exchange thus offered a space for a conversation across intellectual and political geographies. The dispute over "human nature" seemed to crystallize the differences in approach—at once linguistic, philosophical, and political—in the work of Chomsky and Foucault and in their respective countries.

In what ways had the study of language or of discourse prepared each man for his new political role? What, in other words, is the relation between linguistics and politics or the role of power in the analysis of discourse? In some sense, that was a crux of the debate, with each man trying to translate the basic question in his own terms. Is it a matter of linguistic universals and their relation to human justice and decency, as Chomsky argued; or is it, as Foucault maintained, a case of historical and material restrictions on what is said and in their relations with the exercise of power? After some polite attempts to find common ground, a divergence broke out on this score, which, as usual in such exchanges, was ultimately left unresolved. As the decade wore on both men would continue to examine the relation between linguistics and politics, language and power, as they increasingly assumed the role of political intellectuals. Their later reflections serve to amplify the positions in the initial exchange as well as the divergences and links between them. In particular, reproduced in this volume following the debate are attempts each made in 1976 to clarify and elaborate their views (Chapters 2–4). Also included is a lecture given by Foucault at Stanford University in 1978 (Chapter 5), as well as a brief statement (Chapter 6), which originally appeared in the French newspaper *Libération* in 1984, shortly before Foucault's death. These later texts can be read as a kind of aftermath and continuation of the 1971 debate at a time when both men already sensed a reaction against or "falling off" of the earlier possibilities, but also their elaboration in new lines. They deepen the earlier exchange, complicating its terms and reception. As in that earlier debate, these additional chapters retain the informal nature in which each man, moving from his area of expertise or research, addresses a larger public, through interview or lecture, thus reflecting his own passage from academic study to public political activity.

The interviews with Chomsky on politics and language (Chapters 2 and 3) prolong the peculiar mix of English and French in the 1971 debate. Conducted in 1976, they were originally published in France in a volume titled *Dialogues avec Mitsou Ronat.*[2] Ronat, a noted French linguist, asked questions in French; Chomsky responded in English, and the tape-recorded results were then translated into French. In the English-language edition, published in 1979 as *Language and Responsibility* and reissued more recently together with an earlier work by Chomsky as *On Language*, Chomsky introduced "a number of stylistic and sometimes substantive changes" such that the text, in his words, "while preserving the basic structure of the original, is not simply a translation of the French translation of my remarks, but is rather an elaboration and in some cases modification of the French version."[3] The result gives what the translator working with Chomsky believed to be "the clearest exposition yet of Chomsky's basic conception in linguistics and related issues. . . ."[4] Interestingly, in the second dialogue (Chapter 3), Chomsky explicitly recalls his 1971 debate with Foucault, after declaring, "I do not believe that Marxist philosophy, of whatever tendency, has made a substantial contribution to the kind of questions we have been discussing."[5] In the intervening years, the issue of politics and language had been much discussed, and Mitsou Ronat was keen to pose questions to Chomsky about these developments—about the study of totalitarian language by Jean-Pierre Faye, for example, or about the analysis of non-standard English by William Labov. In each case, Chomsky defends his program of "innate" universals. Referring to Labov's study of black English, he says, ". . . I do not see in what way the study of ghetto dialects differs from the study of the dialects of university-trained speakers, from a purely linguistic point of view."[6] He does, however, admit that "no individual speaks a well-defined language," such that the national or "natural" languages studied by linguists are a homogenizing abstraction, an idealization, although nevertheless the condition of "rational" study of language. This is a point with which Gilles Deleuze took issue at the time, suggesting that black English, unlike that of academics, involves another "minor" politics in language-use, which in turn entails a "pragmatic" element, irreducible to the competence-performance distinction in Chomsky's "rational" abstraction.[7]

How do such ideas bear on the disagreement with Foucault concerning language in the earlier Dutch debate? There the discussion had focused on the question of "creativity." Chomsky was impressed by the potentially infinite sentences any child learns to generate in the "natural" language to which he or she is exposed. He argued that the actual verbal evidence at the child's disposal in acquiring such "normal creativity" cannot be inferred simply from verbal clues the child encounters, as Skinner falsely presumed. One needs rather to postulate an innate capacity, akin to the question of "innate ideas" in Descartes. By contrast, Foucault was impressed by the fact that, of the many utterances "normal creativity" allows for, only a very few are actually uttered (spoken or written), and those that are fall into discernable patterns of a time and place. Foucault was interested in *les choses dites.* He imagined there were rules or "regularities" in what is said at a given time and place, and that these rules govern not just the kinds of things that are talked about, but also the roles and positions of those talking about them. He argued that such historical regularities in utterance cannot be explained by innate structures in the minds or brains of language-learners or indeed by any innate predetermination. Neither innate nor learned, they instead condition and constrain the actual use or exercise of our minds across a series of practices, at once material and institutional. In particular, they can be shown to govern the ways in which we talk about language itself, and the ways it is so delimited as to become a "rational" object of study in different periods—as, for example, with the turn from a focus on historical language groups to language "structures." The question of "ideas" in classical philosophy thus needs to be posed in another way, and Foucault offers Chomsky the observation that while the mind in Descartes is not in fact creative but is rather "illuminated by evidence," in Leibniz one finds a picture of the mind "folded back" so as to develop potentials or "virtualities" by unfolding itself in the world, with which the theme of "creativity" might better be associated. Today, there no more exist accepted rules for such "anonymous" regularities in things said than there is anything like a "generative grammar" for any natural language, not even English; but the differing views over the concept of "creativity" nevertheless remain philosophically suggestive. In Foucault's case, it leads to a particular problem: how then do new ways of talking arise? What are the presuppositions and the politics of such non-normal creativity in our forms of discourse?

How did this disagreement figure into the problem of the relation of language-study to politics in the two thinkers? Chomsky begins his dialogue with Mitsou Ronat on this topic by declaring that the specialized knowledge he possesses as a linguist "has no immediate bearing on social and political issues" nor should it. In other words, no special expertise is needed; anyone can engage in political analysis if open-minded and willing to establish the facts with the available information. All that is needed is "Cartesian common sense, which is quite evenly distributed."[8] The possible link between universals of language and international justice is an abstruse matter, which doesn't seem to affect this democratic presupposition of critical thought. This common-sensical approach in turn matches with Chomsky's optimistic view of technology in disseminating information, which he advanced in the earlier debate with Foucault, and which, according to him, "implies that relevant information and relevant understanding can be brought to everyone quickly."[9] Universal linguistics gives us each a "normal creativity" that we are free to exercise through common-sensical study, conveyed to everyone quickly through advanced media. That Chomsky became better known in

France for his political writings than for his work in linguistics seems consistent with this view of the relation between linguistics and politics.

Foucault followed a rather different path in the 1970s. He saw 1968 not simply as a crisis in the university but also as a crisis in knowledge and in particular the knowledge of academic specialists in relation to the new questions thrown up by such events. One needed a new image of the intellectual and new ways of talking about and seeing things, centered on questions of truth and power. His interviews in Italy with Fontana and Pasquino (Chapter 4), conducted in 1976, are not simply an attempt to recast the new struggles in terms of truth and power, but, as in a related interview in France,[10] to introduce a distinction between "specific" and "universal" intellectuals—a tradition of Voltaire, Zola, and Sartre, appealing to higher values as moral conscience for society, and another one exemplified by J. Robert Oppenheimer, concerned as he was with the consequences of the knowledge he helped to develop. It was just this type of "specific" activity that Foucault himself had tried to put into practice, starting with the formation of GIP (*Le Groupe d'Information sur les Prisons*) in February of 1971 (prior to his debate with Chomsky) as a new kind of collective that was rather different from the Maoist groups at the time or from university departmentalization.[11] GIP collected information about prison conditions in France, not simply in an investigative or journalistic manner to present in the media, but as part of a deeper analysis or "diagnosis"—as part of a larger attempt to create new ways of thinking about and viewing the operations of prisons, which Foucault would further develop and present in 1975 in his book *Discipline and Punish*. It was not a simple case of information that was obvious to anyone or easily conveyed through the media; it was closer to attempts, following 1968, by Marcel Ophüls and Jean-Luc Godard (notably in his 1976 television program "Six fois deux") to challenge the media presentation of history and events, exposing exclusions, and introducing other questions.[12] For Foucault, the basic problem was less a shift from Marxist "theology" to Cartesian common-sense as much as the invention or "fabrication" of a new sort of link between politics and truth and speaking-the-truth, for which one needed to develop the model as well as the practice. One needed to break with the "self-evidence" that governs our habits and practices of talking about and seeing things—as, for example, with the "self-evidence" that our prisons serve to "reform" or simply to enforce laws. The aim of Foucault's "analyses of discourse," more than making information publicly available, was an attempt to interrupt and "problematize" things taken for granted in our habits of thinking, and so to suggest other possibilities, to be developed in public discussions—other ways of conceiving of and amplifying questions posed to "politics as usual" and the expertise that supports it, thus opening it up to experimentation. (There is a whole aspect of civil disobedience, discussed in the debate with Chomsky, not only with Martin Luther King Jr. but also with Gandhi, that may be understood in this way—the peculiar force of "speaking the truth" in "problematizing" what is taken for granted in law or justice, releasing possibilities that extended beyond the civil rights movement itself.)

In 1976, while Chomsky was carrying on his dialogues with Mitsou Ronat in France, Foucault, for his part, was working on a new set of concerns, which he would later present in America in his lectures at Stanford (Chapter 5). The recent publication in English of his 1975–76 lecture-course at the Collège de

France, *"Society Must be Defended,"* gives a good idea of these concerns.[13] In these lectures, Foucault was interested in questions of security and populations, welfare and warfare, in the kind of "political rationality" supposed by our governments and the kind of expert and expertise on which they "self-evidently" rely—what Foucault was provisionally calling "bio-power" (in contrast to sovereign power). It is the nature and consequences of such "political rationality" that is the topic of his lectures at Stanford, delivered to a Californian audience, no longer in French, in which Foucault moves toward a kind of "an-archic" element in politics and the struggles that support them—there is an irreducible agonistic element in politics which subsists simply because there can be no pre-existing knowledge of it. It is not, as with earlier socialist models, that a just or decent society is contained in this one in a way that we need only bring to the light of general consciousness; rather it is unforeseen events that cause us to rethink our political habits, introducing new ways of thinking and seeing, requiring originality or "creativity" in ways of speaking, in posing questions *to* politics and the forms of "political rationality" on which it rests.

The problem of power thus extends into questions of justice raised by Chomsky at the end of the original exchange with Foucault. In what way do we find this sort of political possibility in the actual institutions and discourses of justice, and so in the very idea of justice itself? It was a problem that deeply interested Foucault, who hoped to work on it in collaboration with Robert Badinter, a participant in GIP and later Minister of Justice in France.[14] What mattered in the study they envisaged was "juridical discourse" and jurisprudential practices, the larger body of knowledge and practice associated with them, and the events that "problematize" and change them.

The question of "rights" might be understood in this way—civil rights deriving from the revolutionary "problematization" of aristocratic ones; social rights emerging from new knowledge of social and labor conditions and the struggles related to them; and so forth. In the end the nature and guarantee of such rights rests on political grounds and the "practices of truth" associated with them, the new forces that challenge them—as, for Foucault, with the new forces confronting the postwar European "welfare-warfare" state and the kind of political thinking with which it was linked, the kinds of knowledge or expertise it took for granted, which required new ways of thinking—a new "creativity" in thinking. Foucault's remarks in 1984 on human rights and humanitarian interventions (Chapter 6), posed by the "bio-political" state, belong to this view of political activity, linking it to the larger question of an international or "transnational" citizenship of all who "share a difficulty in enduring what is taking place."

Foucault's death later that year deprived us of his continuing role in the discussion. But the moment of interference, exchange, and translation—refracted in the debate with Chomsky over "human nature" almost thirty-five years ago—remains exemplary, not simply in its "transnational" character, moving back and forth between French and English, but also in its illumination of the need, in relation to current and pressing issues, for the ongoing collective exercise of different kinds of "philosophical intelligence" in the face of what is taking place.

—John Rajchman
May 2006
New York City

Notes

1. Chomsky later reported that the two had lively discussions off air as well.
2. Noam Chomsky, *Dialogues avec Mitsou Ronat* (Paris: Flammarion, 1977).
3. Noam Chomsky, *Language and Responsibility* (New York: Pantheon, 1979); *On Language* (New York: The New Press, 1998), p. ix.
4. Ibid, p. viii.
5. See Chapter 3, p. 131 in the present volume.
6. Noam Chomsky, *On Language* (New York: The New Press, 1998), pp. 53–54.
7. Gilles Deleuze et al., *Dialogues* (New York: Columbia University Press, 2002). These remarks are elaborated in *A Thousand Plateaus* (Minneapolis: University of Minnesota Press, 1987), where Deleuze and Guattari spell out their objections to Chomsky's "homogenizing abstraction" and advance their opposing conception of the pragmatics of "minor languages" (see especially pp. 102–3).
8. See Chapter 2, p. 70 in the present volume.
9. See Chapter 1, p. 64 in the present volume.
10. Michel Foucault, "La fonction politique de l'intellectuel," *Politique-Hebdo*, November 29–December 5, 1976; reproduced in *Dits et écrits* (Paris: Éditions Gallimard, 1994), III, pp. 109–114.
11. For an account of the formation of GIP, see Daniel Defert's "Chronologie" in *Dits et écrits* (Paris: Éditions Gallimard, 1994), III, pp. 37ff. It is interesting to note Foucault's increasing distance from Mao and Maoism in forming GIP and following the publication of Simon Leys's 1971 book, *Les habits neufs du president Mao*, which was critical of him. The archives of GIP were recently published in France as *Le groupe d'information sur les prisons* (Paris: Éditions de l'Imec, 2005).
12. For a brief account of the impact of 1968 on television in France,

see Jill Forbes's entry "Television" in *The Columbia History of Twentieth-Century French Thought*, ed. Lawrence D. Kritzman (New York: Columbia University Press, 2005), pp. 740ff; Gilles Deleuze reviewed Godard's "Six fois deux" in *Negotiations* (New York: Columbia University Press, 1997); Deleuze came to contrast the peculiar "time" of "events" explored in the work of Ophüls and Godard with the "present" of television and its tendency to turn us into passive spectators, or worse, voyeurs of what is happening to us.

13. Michel Foucault, *"Society Must Be Defended"* (New York: Picador, 2003). The consequences of these views for an analysis of liberalism (and neo-liberalism) as a kind of "political rationality" is explored in Foucault's *Naissance de la biopolitique* (Paris: Éditions Gallimard, 2005).

14. In a short testimony published after his death, Robert Badinter remembers meetings and encounters with Foucault over their "common horizon . . . Justice"; he recalls the clipped clarity and brilliance of Foucault's words and his peculiar passion to "reveal the unknown behind the too-well-known" ("Au nom des mots" in *Michel Foucault: une histoire de la verite*; Syros, 1985, pp. 73–5). The two had been invited by Pierre Nora for a public debate on the social function of punishment to prepare for the formation of a multi-disciplinary research group on "the secret functions and actual practice" of the rule of law, which Foucault had likened to a "flying buttress" holding together opposing forces. The project was cut off by Foucault's hospitalization and death. As Minister of Justice, Badinter would take the initiative abolishing the death penalty (against majority French opinion), a position Foucault defended against the views of psychoanalysts like Jean Laplanche, concerned with the Father and the Symbolic Order. For Foucault, the death penalty was rather to be understood in terms of the new role of death in the "biopolitical" formation he was attempting to delineate (see *The History of Sexuality*; New York: Vintage, 1980, pp. 137–8).

THE CHOMSKY-FOUCAULT DEBATE

1.

Human Nature: Justice vs. Power

A Debate Between Noam Chomsky and Michel Foucault

FONS ELDERS: Ladies and gentlemen, welcome to the third debate of the International Philosophers' Project. Tonight's debaters are Mr. Michel Foucault, of the Collège de France, and Mr. Noam Chomsky, of the Massachusetts Institute of Technology. Both philosophers have points in common and points of difference. Perhaps the best way to compare both philosophers would be to see them as tunnellers through a mountain working at opposite sides of the same mountain with different tools, without even knowing if they are working in each other's direction.

But both are doing their jobs with quite new ideas, digging as profoundly as possible with an equal commitment in philosophy as in politics: enough reasons, it seems to me, for us to expect a fascinating debate about philosophy and about politics.

I intend, therefore, not to lose any time and to start off with a central, perennial question: the question of human nature.

All studies of man, from history to linguistics and psychology, are faced with the question of whether, in the last instance, we are the product of all kinds of external factors, or if, in spite of our differences, we have something we could call a common human nature, by which we can recognize each other as human beings.

So my first question is to you, Mr. Chomsky, because you often employ the concept of human nature, in which connection you even use terms like "innate ideas" and "innate structures." Which arguments can you derive from linguistics to give such a central position to this concept of human nature?

NOAM CHOMSKY: Well, let me begin in a slightly technical way.

A person who is interested in studying languages is faced with a very definite empirical problem. He's faced with an organism, a mature, let's say adult, speaker, who has somehow acquired an amazing range of abilities, which enable him in particular to say what he means, to understand what people say to him, to do this in a fashion that I think is proper to call highly creative . . . that is, much of what a person says in his normal intercourse with others is novel, much of what you hear is new, it doesn't bear any close resemblance to anything in your experience; it's not random novel behaviour, clearly, it's behaviour which is in some sense which is very hard to characterize, appropriate to situations. And in fact it has many of the characteristics of what I think might very well be called creativity.

Now, the person who has acquired this intricate and highly articulated and organized collection of abilities—the collection of abilities that we call knowing a language—has been exposed to a certain experience; he has been presented in the course of his lifetime with a certain amount of data, of direct experience with a language.

We can investigate the data that's available to this person; having done so, in principle, we're faced with a reasonably clear and well-delineated scientific problem, namely that of accounting for the gap between the really quite small quantity of data, small and rather degenerate in quality, that's presented to the child, and the very highly articulated, highly systematic, profoundly organized resulting knowledge that he somehow derives from these data.

Furthermore we notice that varying individuals with very varied experience in a particular language nevertheless arrive at systems which are very much congruent to one another. The systems that two speakers of English arrive at on the basis of their very different experiences are congruent in the sense that, over an overwhelming range, what one of them says, the other can understand.

Furthermore, even more remarkable, we notice that in a wide range of languages, in fact all that have been studied seriously, there are remarkable limitations on the kind of systems that emerge from the very different kinds of experiences to which people are exposed.

There is only one possible explanation, which I have to give in a rather schematic fashion, for this remarkable phenomenon, namely the assumption that the individual himself contributes a good deal, an overwhelming part in fact, of the general schematic structure and perhaps even of the specific content of the knowledge that he ultimately derives from this very scattered and limited experience.

A person who knows a language has acquired that knowledge because he approached the learning experience with a very explicit and detailed schematism that tells him what kind of language it is that he is being exposed to. That is, to put it rather loosely: the child must begin with the knowledge, certainly not with the knowledge that he's hearing English or Dutch or French or something else, but he *does* start with the knowledge that he's hearing a human language of a very narrow and explicit type, that permits a very small range of variation. And it is because he begins with that highly organized and very restrictive schematism, that he is able to make the huge leap from scattered and degenerate data to highly organized knowledge. And furthermore I should add that we can go a certain distance, I think a rather long distance, towards presenting the properties of this system of knowledge, that I would call innate language or instinctive knowledge, that the child brings to language learning; and also we can go a long way towards describing the system that is mentally represented when he has acquired this knowledge.

I would claim then that this instinctive knowledge, if you like, this schematism that makes it possible to derive complex and intricate knowledge on the basis of very partial data, is one fundamental constituent of human nature. In this case I think a fundamental constituent because of the role that language plays, not merely in communication, but also in expression of thought and interaction between persons; and I assume that in other domains of human intelligence, in other domains of human cognition and behavior, something of the same sort must be true.

Well, this collection, this mass of schematisms, innate organizing principles, which guides our social and intellectual and individual behavior, that's what I mean to refer to by the concept of human nature.

ELDERS: Well, Mr. Foucault, when I think of your books like *The History of Madness* and *Words and Objects*, I get the impression that you are working on a completely different level and with a totally opposite aim and goal; when I think of the word *schematism* in relation to human nature, I suppose you are trying to elaborate several periods with several schematisms. What do you say to this?

MICHEL FOUCAULT: Well, if you don't mind I will answer in French, because my English is so poor that I would be ashamed of answering in English.

It is true that I mistrust the notion of human nature a little, and for the following reason: I believe that of the concepts or notions which a science can use, not all have the same degree of elaboration, and that in general they have neither the same function nor the same type of possible use in scientific discourse. Let's take the example of biology. You will find concepts with a classifying function, concepts with a differentiating function, and concepts with an analytical function: some of them enable us to characterize objects, for example that of "tissue"; others to isolate elements, like that of "hereditary feature"; others to fix relations, such as that of "reflex." There are at the same time elements which play a role in the discourse and in the internal rules of the reasoning practice. But there also exist "peripheral" notions, those by which scientific practice designates itself, differentiates itself in relation to other practices, delimits its domain of objects, and designates what it considers to be the totality of its future tasks. The notion of life played this role to some extent in biology during a certain period.

In the seventeenth and eighteenth centuries, the notion of life was hardly used in studying nature: one classified natural beings, whether living or non-living, in a vast hierarchical tableau which went from minerals to man; the break between the minerals and the plants or animals was relatively undecided; epistemologically it was only important to fix their positions once and for all in an indisputable way.

At the end of the eighteenth century, the description and analysis of these natural beings showed, through the use of more highly perfected instruments and the latest techniques, an entire domain of objects, an entire field of relations and processes which have enabled us to define the specificity of biology in the knowledge of nature. Can one say that research into life has finally constituted itself in biological science? Has the concept of life been responsible for the organization of biological knowledge? I don't think so. It seems to me more likely that the transformations of biological knowledge at the end of the eighteenth century were demonstrated on one hand by a whole series of new concepts for use in scientific discourse and on the other hand gave rise to a notion like that of life which has enabled us to designate, to delimit, and to situate a certain type of scientific discourse, among other things. I would say that the notion of life is not a *scientific concept*; it has been an *epistemological indicator* of which the classifying, delimiting, and other functions had an effect on scientific discussions, and not on what they were talking about.

Well, it seems to me that the notion of human nature is of the same type. It was not by studying human nature that linguists discovered the laws of consonant mutation, or Freud the principles of the analysis of dreams, or cultural anthropologists the structure of myths. In the history of knowledge, the notion of human nature seems to me mainly to have played the role of an epistemological indicator to designate certain types of discourse in relation to or in opposition to theology or biology or history. I would find it difficult to see in this a scientific concept.

CHOMSKY: Well, in the first place, if we were able to specify in terms of, let's say, neural networks the properties of human cognitive structure that make it possible for the child to acquire these complicated systems, then I at least would have no hesitation in describing those properties as being a constituent element of human nature. That is, there is something biologically given, unchangeable, a foundation for whatever it is that we do with our mental capacities in this case.

But I would like to pursue a little further the line of development that you outlined, with which in fact I entirely agree, about the concept of life as an organizing concept in the biological sciences.

It seems to me that one might speculate a bit further— speculate in this case, since we're talking about the future, not the past—and ask whether the concept of human nature or of innate organizing mechanisms or of intrinsic mental schematism or whatever we want to call it, I don't see much difference between them, but let's call it human nature for shorthand, might not provide for biology the next peak to try to scale, after having—at least in the minds of the biologists, though one might perhaps question this—already answered to the satisfaction of some the question of what is life.

In other words, to be precise, is it possible to give a biological explanation or a physical explanation . . . is it possible to characterize, in terms of the physical concepts presently available to us, the ability of the child to acquire complex systems of knowledge; and furthermore, critically, having acquired such systems of knowledge, to make use of this knowledge in the free and creative and remarkably varied ways in which he does?

Can we explain in biological terms, ultimately in physical terms, these properties of both acquiring knowledge in the first place and making use of it in the second? I really see no reason to believe that we can; that is, it's an article of faith on the part of scientists that since science has explained many other things it will also explain this.

In a sense one might say that this is a variant of the body–mind problem. But if we look back at the way in which science has scaled various peaks, and at the way in which the concept of life was finally acquired by science after having been beyond its vision for a long period, then I think we notice at many points in history—and in fact the seventeenth and eighteenth centuries are particularly clear examples—that scientific advances were possible precisely because the domain of physical science was itself enlarged. Classic cases are Newton's gravitational forces. To the Cartesians, action at a distance was a mystical concept, and in fact to Newton himself it was an occult quality, a mystical entity, which didn't belong within science. To the common sense of a later generation, action at a distance has been incorporated within science.

What happened was that the notion of body, the notion of the physical had changed. To a Cartesian, a strict Cartesian, if such a person appeared today, it would appear that there is no explanation for the behavior of the heavenly bodies. Certainly there is no explanation for the phenomena that are explained in terms of electro-magnetic force, let's say. But by the extension of physical science to incorporate hitherto unavailable concepts, entirely new ideas, it became possible to successively build more and more complicated structures that incorporated a larger range of phenomena.

For example, it's certainly not true that the physics of the Cartesians is able to explain, let's say, the behavior of elementary particles in physics, just as it's unable to explain the concepts of life.

Similarly, I think, one might ask the question whether physical science as known today, including biology, incorporates within itself the principles and the concepts that will enable it to give an account of innate human intellectual capacities and, even more profoundly, of the ability to make use of those capacities under conditions of freedom in the way which humans do. I see no particular reason to believe that biology or physics now contain those concepts, and it may be that to scale the next peak, to make the next step, they will have to focus on this organizing concept, and may very well have to broaden their scope in order to come to grips with it.

ELDERS: Perhaps I may try to ask one more specific question leading out of both your answers, because I'm afraid otherwise the debate will become too technical. I have the impression that one of the main differences between you both has its origin in a difference in approach. You, Mr. Foucault, are especially interested in the way science or scientists function in a certain period, whereas Mr. Chomsky is more interested in the so-called "what-questions": why we possess language—not just how language functions, but what's the *reason* for our having language. We can try to elucidate this in a more general way: you, Mr. Foucault, are delimiting eighteenth-century rationalism, whereas you, Mr. Chomsky, are combining eighteenth-century rationalism with notions like freedom and creativity.

Perhaps we could illustrate this in a more general way with examples from the seventeenth and eighteenth centuries.

CHOMSKY: Well, first I should say that I approach classical rationalism not really as a historian of science or a historian of philosophy, but from the rather different point of view of someone who has a certain range of scientific notions and is interested in seeing how at an earlier stage people may have been groping towards these notions, possibly without even realizing what they were groping towards.

So one might say that I'm looking at history not as an antiquarian, who is interested in finding out and giving a precisely accurate account of what the thinking of the seventeenth century was—I don't mean to demean that activity, it's just not mine—but rather from the point of view of, let's say, an art lover, who wants to look at the seventeenth century to find in it things that are of particular value, and that obtain part of their value in part because of the perspective with which he approaches them.

And I think that, without objecting to the other approach, my approach is legitimate; that is, I think it is perfectly possible to go back to earlier stages of scientific thinking on the basis of our present understanding, and to perceive how great thinkers were, within the limitations of their time, groping toward concepts and ideas and insights that they themselves could not be clearly aware of.

For example, I think that anyone can do this about his own thought. Without trying to compare oneself to the great thinkers of the past, anyone can consider what he now knows and can ask what he knew twenty years ago, and can see that in some unclear fashion he was striving towards something which he can only now understand . . . if he is fortunate.

Similarly I think it's possible to look at the past, without distorting your view, and it is in these terms that I want to look at the seventeenth century. Now, when I look back at the seventeenth and eighteenth centuries, what strikes me particularly is the way in which, for example, Descartes and his followers were led to postulate mind as a thinking substance independent of the body. If you look at their reasons for postulating this second substance, mind, thinking entity, they were that Descartes was able to convince himself, rightly or wrongly, it doesn't matter at the moment, that events in the physical world and even much of the behavioral and psychological world, for example a good deal of sensation, were explicable in terms of what he considered to be physics—wrongly, as we now believe—that is, in terms of things bumping into each other and turning and moving and so on.

He thought that in those terms, in terms of the mechanical principle, he could explain a certain domain of phenomena; and then he observed that there was a range of phenomena that he argued could not be explained in those terms. And he therefore postulated a creative principle to account for that domain of phenomena, the principle of mind with its own properties. And then later followers, many who didn't regard themselves as

Cartesians, for example many who regarded themselves as strongly anti-rationalistic, developed the concept of creation within a system of rule.

I won't bother with the details, but my own research into the subject led me ultimately to Wilhelm von Humboldt, who certainly didn't consider himself a Cartesian, but nevertheless in a rather different framework and within a different historical period and with different insight, in a remarkable and ingenious way, which, I think, is of lasting importance, also developed the concept of internalized form—fundamentally the concept of free creation within a system of rule—in an effort to come to grips with some of the same difficulties and problems that the Cartesians faced in their terms.

Now I believe, and here I would differ from a lot of my colleagues, that the move of Descartes to the postulation of a second substance was a very scientific move; it was not a metaphysical or an anti-scientific move. In fact, in many ways it was very much like Newton's intellectual move when he postulated action at a distance; he was moving into the domain of the occult, if you like. He was moving into the domain of something that went beyond well-established science, and was trying to integrate it with well-established science by developing a theory in which these notions could be properly clarified and explained.

Now Descartes, I think, made a similar intellectual move in postulating a second substance. Of course he failed where Newton succeeded; that is, he was unable to lay the groundworks for a mathematical theory of mind, as achieved by Newton and his followers, which laid the groundwork for a mathematical theory of physical entities that incorporated such occult notions as action at a distance and later electro-magnetic forces and so on.

But then that poses for us, I think, the task of carrying on and developing this, if you like, mathematical theory of mind; by that I simply mean a precisely articulated, clearly formulated, abstract theory which will have empirical consequences, which will let us know whether the theory is right or wrong, or on the wrong track or the right track, and at the same time will have the properties of mathematical science, that is, the properties of rigor and precision and a structure that makes it possible for us to deduce conclusions from assumptions and so on.

Now it's from that point of view that I try to look back at the seventeenth and eighteenth centuries and to pick out points, which I think are really there, even though I certainly recognize, and in fact would want to insist, that the individuals in question may not have seen it this way.

ELDERS: Mr. Foucault, I suppose you will have a severe criticism of this?

FOUCAULT: No . . . there are just one or two little historical points. I cannot object to the account which you have given in your historical analysis of their reasons and of their modality. But there is one thing one could nevertheless add: when you speak of creativity as conceived by Descartes, I wonder if you don't transpose to Descartes an idea which is to be found among his successors or even certain of his contemporaries. According to Descartes, the mind was not so very creative. It saw, it perceived, it was illuminated by the evidence.

Moreover, the problem which Descartes never resolved

nor entirely mastered was that of understanding how one could pass from one of these clear and distinct ideas, one of these intuitions, to another, and what status should be given to the evidence of the passage between them. I can't see exactly either the creation in the moment where the mind grasped the truth for Descartes, or even the real creation in the passage from one truth to another.

On the contrary, you can find, I think, at the same time in Pascal and Leibniz, something which is much closer to what you are looking for: in other words in Pascal and in the whole Augustinian stream of Christian thought, you find this idea of a mind in profundity; of a mind folded back in the intimacy of itself which is touched by a sort of unconsciousness, and which can develop its potentialities by the deepening of the self. And that is why the grammar of Port-Royal, to which you refer, is, I think, much more Augustinian than Cartesian.

And furthermore you will find in Leibniz something which you will certainly like: the idea that in the profundity of the mind is incorporated a whole web of logical relations which constitutes, in a certain sense, the rational unconscious of the consciousness, the not yet clarified and visible form of the reason itself, which the monad or the individual develops little by little, and with which he understands the whole world.

That's where I would make a very small criticism.

ELDERS: Mr. Chomsky, one moment please.

I don't think it's a question of making a historical criticism, but of formulating your own opinions on these quite fundamental concepts. . . .

FOUCAULT: But one's fundamental opinions can be demonstrated in precise analyses such as these.

ELDERS: Yes, all right. But I remember some passages in your *History of Madness*, which give a description of the seventeenth and eighteenth centuries in terms of repression, suppression, and exclusion, while for Mr. Chomsky this period is full of creativity and individuality.

Why do we have at that period, for the first time, closed psychiatric or insane asylums? I think this is a very fundamental question. . . .

FOUCAULT: . . . on creativity, yes!

But I don't know, perhaps Mr. Chomsky would like to speak about it . . .

ELDERS: No, no, no, please go on. Continue.

FOUCAULT: No, I would like to say this: in the historical studies that I have been able to make, or have tried to make, I have without any doubt given very little room to what you might call the creativity of individuals, to their capacity for creation, to their aptitude for inventing by themselves, for originating concepts, theories, or scientific truths by themselves.

But I believe that my problem is different to that of Mr. Chomsky. Mr. Chomsky has been fighting against linguistic behaviorism, which attributed almost nothing to the creativity of the speaking subject; the speaking subject was a kind of surface on which information came together little by little, which he afterwards combined.

In the field of the history of science or, more generally, the history of thought, the problem was completely different.

The history of knowledge has tried for a long time to obey two claims. One is the claim of *attribution:* each discovery should not only be situated and dated, but should also be attributed to someone; it should have an inventor and someone responsible for it. General or collective phenomena on the other hand, those which by definition can't be "attributed," are normally devalued: they are still traditionally described through words like *tradition, mentality, modes;* and one lets them play the negative role of a brake in relation to the "originality" of the inventor. In brief, this has to do with the principle of the sovereignty of the subject applied to the history of knowledge. The other claim is that which no longer allows us to save the subject, but the truth: so that it won't be compromised by history, it is necessary not that the truth constitutes itself in history, but only that it reveals itself in it; hidden to men's eyes, provisionally inaccessible, sitting in the shadows, it will wait to be unveiled. The history of truth would be essentially its delay, its fall, or the disappearance of the obstacles which have impeded it until now from coming to light. The historical dimension of knowledge is always negative in relation to the truth. It isn't difficult to see how these two claims were adjusted, one to the other: the phenomena of collective order, the "common thought," the "prejudices" of the "myths" of a period, constituted the obstacles which the subject of knowledge had to surmount or to outlive in order to have access finally to the truth; he had to be in an "eccentric" position in order to "discover." At one level this seems to be invoking a certain "romanticism" about the history of science: the solitude of the man of truth, the originality which reopened itself onto the original through history and despite it. I think that, more fundamentally, it's a matter of superimposing the theory of knowledge and the subject of knowledge on the history of knowledge.

And what if understanding the relation of the subject to the truth were just an effect of knowledge? What if understanding were a complex, multiple, non-individual formation, not "subjected to the subject," which produced effects of truth? One should then put forward positively this entire dimension which the history of science has negativized, analyze the productive capacity of knowledge as a collective practice, and consequently replace individuals and their "knowledge" in the development of a knowledge which at a given moment functions according to certain rules which one can register and describe.

You will say to me that all the Marxist historians of science have been doing this for a long time. But when one sees how they work with these facts and especially what use they make of the notions of consciousness, of ideology as opposed to science, one realizes that they are for the main part more or less detached from the theory of knowledge.

In any case, what I am anxious about is substituting transformations of the understanding for the history of the discoveries of knowledge. Therefore I have, in appearance at least, a completely different attitude to Mr. Chomsky apropos creativity, because for me it is a matter of effacing the dilemma of the knowing subject, while for him it is a matter of allowing the dilemma of the speaking subject to reappear.

But if he has made it reappear, if he has described it, it is because he can do so. The linguists have for a long time now analyzed language as a system with a collective value. The understanding as a collective totality of rules allowing such and such a knowledge to be produced in a certain period, has hardly been studied until now. Nevertheless, it presents some fairly positive characteristics to the observer. Take for example medicine at the end of the eighteenth century: read twenty medical works, it doesn't matter which, of the years 1770 to 1780, then twenty others from the years 1820 to 1830, and I would say, quite at random, that in forty or fifty years everything had changed; what one talked about, the way one talked about it, not just the remedies, of course, not just the maladies and their classifications, but the outlook itself. Who was responsible for that? Who was the author of it? It is artificial, I think, to say Bichat, or even to expand a little and to say the first anatomical clinicians. It's a matter of a collective and complex transformation of medical understanding in its practice and its rules. And this transformation is far from a negative phenomenon: it is the suppression of a negativity, the effacement of an obstacle, the disappearance of prejudices, the abandonment of old myths, the retreat of irrational beliefs, and access finally freed to experience and to reason; it represents the application of an entirely new *grille* [grid], with its choices and exclusions; a new play with its own rules, decisions, and limitations, with its own inner logic, its parameters, and its blind alleys, all of which lead to the modification of the point of origin. And it is in this functioning that the understanding itself exists. So, if one studies the history of knowledge, one sees that there are two broad directions of analysis: according to one, one has to show how, under what conditions, and for what reasons the understanding modifies itself in its formative rules, without passing through an original "inventor" discovering the "truth"; and according to the other, one has to show how the working of the rules of an understanding can produce in an individual new and unpublished knowledge. Here my aim rejoins, with imperfect methods and in a quite inferior mode, Mr. Chomsky's project: accounting for the fact that with a few rules or definite elements, unknown totalities, never even produced, can be brought to light by individuals. To resolve this problem, Mr. Chomsky has to reintroduce the dilemma of the subject in the field of grammatical analysis. To resolve an analogous problem in the field of history with which I am involved, one has to do the opposite, in a way: to introduce the point of view of understanding, of its rules, of its systems, of its transformations of totalities in the game of individual knowledge. Here and there the problem of creativity cannot be resolved in the same way, or rather, it can't be formulated in the same terms, given the state of disciplines inside which it is put.

CHOMSKY: I think in part we're slightly talking at cross purposes, because of a different use of the term *creativity*. In fact, I should say that my use of the term *creativity* is a little bit idiosyncratic, and therefore the onus falls on me in this case, not on you. But when I speak of creativity, I'm not attributing to the concept the notion of value that is normal when we speak of creativity. That is, when you speak of scientific creativity, you're speaking, properly, of the achievements of a Newton. But in the context in which I have been speaking about creativity, it's a normal human act.

I'm speaking of the kind of creativity that any child demonstrates when he's able to come to grips with a new situation: to describe it properly, react to it properly, tell one something about it, think about it in a new fashion for him, and so on. I think it's appropriate to call those acts creative, but of course without thinking of those acts as being the acts of a Newton.

In fact it may very well be *true* that creativity in the arts or the sciences, that which goes beyond the normal, may really involve properties of, well, I would also say of human nature, which may not exist fully developed in the mass of mankind, and may not constitute part of the normal creativity of everyday life.

Now my belief is that science can look forward to the problem of normal creativity as a topic that it can perhaps incorporate within itself. But I don't believe, and I suspect you will agree, that science can look forward, at least in the reasonable future, to coming to grips with true creativity, the achievements of the great artist and the great scientist. It has no hope of accommodating these unique phenomena within its grasp. It's the lower levels of creativity that I've been speaking of.

Now, as far as what you say about the history of science is concerned, I think that's correct and illuminating and particularly relevant, in fact, to the kinds of enterprise that I see lying before us in psychology and linguistics and the philosophy of the mind.

That is, I think there are certain topics that have been repressed or put aside during the scientific advances of the past few centuries.

For example, this concern with low-level creativity that I'm referring to was really present in Descartes also. For example, when he speaks of the difference between a parrot, who can mimic what is said, and a human, who can say new things that are appropriate to the situation, and when he specifies that as being the distinctive property that designates the limits of physics and carries us into the science of the mind, to use modern terms, I think he really is referring to the kind of creativity that I have in mind; and I quite agree with your comments about the other sources of such notions.

Well, these concepts, even in fact the whole notion of the organization of sentence structure, were put aside during the period of great advances that followed from Sir William Jones and others and the development of comparative philology as a whole.

But now, I think, we can go beyond that period when it was necessary to forget and to pretend that these phenomena did not exist and to turn to something else. In this period of comparative philology and also, in my view, structural linguistics, and much of behavioral psychology, and in fact much of what grows out of the empiricist tradition in the study of mind and behavior, it is possible to put aside those limitations and bring into our consideration just those topics that animated a good deal of the thinking and speculation of the seventeenth and eighteenth centuries, and to incorporate them within a much broader and I think deeper science of man that will give a fuller role—though it is certainly not expected to give a complete understanding—to such notions as innovation and creativity and freedom and the production of new entities, new elements of thought and behavior within some system of rule and schematism. Those are concepts that I think we can come to grips with.

ELDERS: Well, may I first of all ask you not to make your answers so lengthy. [*Foucault laughs.*]

When you discuss creativity and freedom, I think that one of the misunderstandings, if any misunderstandings have arisen, has to do with the fact that Mr. Chomsky is starting from a limited number of rules with infinite possibilities of application, whereas you, Mr. Foucault, are stressing the inevitability of the "grille" of our historical and psychological determinisms, which also applies to the way in which we discover new ideas.

Perhaps we can sort this out, not by analyzing the scientific process, but just by analysing our own thought process.

When you discover a new fundamental idea, Mr. Foucault, do you believe that as far as your own personal creativity is concerned, something is happening that makes you feel that you are being liberated, that something new has been developed? Perhaps afterwards you discover that it was not so new. But do you yourself believe that, within your own personality, creativity and freedom are working together, or not?

FOUCAULT: Oh, you know, I don't believe that the problem of personal experience is so very important in a question like this. No, I believe that there is in reality quite a strong similarity between what Mr. Chomsky said and what I tried to show: in other words there exist in fact only possible creations, possible innovations. One can only, in terms of language or of knowledge, produce something new by putting into play a certain number of rules which will define the acceptability or the grammaticality of these statements, or which will define, in the case of knowledge, the scientific character of the statements.

Thus, we can roughly say that linguists before Mr. Chomsky mainly insisted on the rules of construction of statements and less on the innovation represented by every new statement, or the hearing of a new statement. And in the history of science or in the history of thought, we placed more emphasis on individual creation, and we had kept aside and left in the shadows these communal, general rules, which obscurely manifest themselves through every scientific discovery, every scientific invention, and even every philosophical innovation.

And to that degree, when I no doubt wrongly believe that I am saying something new, I am nevertheless conscious of the fact that in my statement there are rules at work, not only linguistic rules, but also epistemological rules, and those rules characterize contemporary knowledge.

CHOMSKY: Well, perhaps I can try to react to those comments within my own framework in a way which will maybe shed some light on this.

Let's think again of a human child, who has in his mind some schematism that determines the kind of language he can learn. Okay. And then, given experience, he very quickly knows the language, of which this experience is a part, or in which it is included.

Now this is a normal act; that is, it's an act of normal intelligence, but it's a highly creative act.

If a Martian were to look at this process of acquiring this vast and complicated and intricate system of knowledge on the basis of this ridiculously small quantity of data, he would think of it as an immense act of invention and creation. In fact, a Martian would, I think, consider it as much of an achievement as the invention of, let's say, any aspect of a physical theory on the basis of the data that was presented to the physicist.

However, if this hypothetical Martian were then to observe that every normal human child immediately carries out this creative act and they all do it in the same way and without any difficulty, whereas it takes centuries of genius to slowly carry out the creative act of going from evidence to a scientific theory, then this Martian would, if he were rational, conclude that the structure of the knowledge that is acquired in the case of language is basically internal to the human mind; whereas the structure of physics is not, in so direct a way, internal to the human mind. Our minds are not constructed so that when we look at the phenomena of the world theoretical physics comes forth, and we write it down and produce it; that's not the way our minds are constructed.

Nevertheless, I think there is a possible point of connection, and it might be useful to elaborate it: that is, how is it that we are able to construct any kind of scientific theory at all? How is it that, given a small amount of data, it's possible for various scientists, for various geniuses even, over a long period of time, to arrive at some kind of a theory, at least in some cases, that is more or less profound and more or less empirically adequate?

This is a remarkable fact.

And, in fact, if it were not the case that these scientists, including the geniuses, were beginning with a very narrow limitation on the class of possible scientific theories, if they didn't have built into their minds somehow an obviously unconscious specification of what is a possible scientific theory, then this inductive leap would certainly be quite impossible: just as if each child did not have built into his mind the concept of human language in a very restricted way, then the inductive leap from data to knowledge of a language would be impossible.

So even though the process of, let's say, deriving knowledge of physics from data is far more complex, far more difficult for an organism such as ours, far more drawn out in time, requiring intervention of genius and so on and so forth, nevertheless in a certain sense the achievement of discovering physical science or biology or whatever you like is based on something rather similar to the achievement of the normal child in discovering the structure of his language: that is, it *must* be achieved on the basis of an initial limitation, an initial restriction on the class of possible theories. If you didn't begin by knowing that only certain things are possible theories, then no induction would be possible at all. You could go from data anywhere, in any direction. And the fact that science converges and progresses itself shows us that such initial limitations and structures exist.

If we really want to develop a theory of scientific creation, or for that matter artistic creation, I think we have to focus attention precisely on that set of conditions that, on the one hand, delimits and restricts the scope of our possible knowledge, while at the same time permitting the inductive leap to complicated systems of knowledge on the basis of a small amount of data. That, it seems to me, would be the way to progress towards a theory of scientific creativity, or in fact towards any question of epistemology.

ELDERS: Well, I think if we take this point of the initial limitation with all its creative possibilities, I have the impression that for Mr. Chomsky rules and freedom are not opposed to each other, but more or less imply each other. Whereas I get the impression that it is just the reverse for you, Mr. Foucault. What are your reasons for putting it the opposite way, for this really is a very fundamental point in the debate, and I hope we can elaborate it.

To formulate the same problem in other terms: can you think of universal knowledge without any form of repression?

FOUCAULT: Well, in what Mr. Chomsky has just said there is something which seems to me to create a little difficulty; perhaps I understood it badly.

I believe that you have been talking about a limited number of possibilities in the order of a scientific theory. That is true if you limit yourself to a fairly short period of time, whatever it may be. But if you consider a longer period, it seems to me that what is striking is the proliferation of possibilities by divergences.

For a long time the idea has existed that the sciences, knowledge, followed a certain line of "progress," obeying the principle of "growth," and the principle of the convergence of all these kinds of knowledge. And yet when one sees how the European understanding, which turned out to be a worldwide and universal understanding in a historical and geographical sense, developed, can one say that there has been growth? I, myself, would say that it has been much more a matter of transformation.

Take, as an example, animal and plant classifications. How often have they not been rewritten since the Middle Ages according to completely different rules: by symbolism, by natural history, by comparative anatomy, by the theory of evolution. Each time this rewriting makes the knowledge completely different in its functions, in its economy, in its internal relations. You have there a principle of divergence, much more than one of growth. I would much rather say that there are many different ways of making possible simultaneously a few types of knowledge. There is, therefore, from a certain point of view, always an excess of *data* in relation to possible systems in a given period, which causes them to be experienced within their boundaries, even in their deficiency, which means that one fails to realize their creativity; and from another point of view, that of the historian, there is an excess, a proliferation of systems for a small amount of *data*, from which originates the widespread idea that it is the discovery of new facts which determines movement in the history of science.

CHOMSKY: Here perhaps again, let me try to synthesize a bit. I agree with your conception of scientific progress; that is, I don't think that scientific progress is simply a matter of the accumulated addition of new knowledge and the absorption of new theories and so on. Rather I think that it has this sort of jagged pattern that you describe, forgetting certain problems and leaping to new theories . . .

FOUCAULT: And transforming the same knowledge.

CHOMSKY: Right. But I think that one can perhaps hazard an explanation for that. Oversimplifying grossly, I really don't mean what I'm going to say now literally, one might suppose that the following general lines of an explanation are accurate: it is as if, as human beings of a particular biologically given organization, we have in our heads, to start with, a certain set of possible intellectual structures, possible sciences. Okay?

Now, in the lucky event that some aspect of reality happens to have the character of one of these structures in our mind, then we have a science: that is to say that, fortunately, the structure of our mind and the structure of some aspect of reality co-incide sufficiently so that we develop an intelligible science.

It is precisely this initial limitation in our minds to a certain kind of possible science which provides the tremendous richness and creativity of scientific knowledge. It is important to stress—and this has to do with your point about limitation and freedom—that were it not for these limitations, we would not have the creative act of going from a little bit of knowledge, a little bit of experience, to a rich and highly articulated and complicated array of knowledge. Because if anything could be possible, then nothing would be possible.

But it is precisely because of this property of our minds, which in detail we don't understand, but which, I think, in a general way we can begin to perceive, which presents us with certain possible intelligible structures, and which in the course of history and insight and experience begins to come into focus or fall out of focus and so on; it is precisely because of this property of our minds that the progress of science, I think, has this erratic and jagged character that you describe.

That doesn't mean that everything is ultimately going to fall within the domain of science. Personally I believe that many of the things we would like to understand, and maybe the things we would *most* like to understand, such as the nature of man, or the nature of a decent society, or lots of other things, might really fall outside the scope of possible human science.

ELDERS: Well, I think that we are confronted again with the question of the inner relation between limitation and freedom. Do you agree, Mr. Foucault, with the statement about the combination of limitation, fundamental limitation . . .

FOUCAULT: It is not a matter of combination. Only creativity is possible in putting into play a system of rules; it is not a mixture of order and freedom.

Where perhaps I don't completely agree with Mr. Chomsky is when he places the principle of these regularities, in a way, in the interior of the mind or of human nature.

If it is a matter of whether these rules are effectively put to work by the human mind, all right; all right, too, if it is a question of whether the historian and the linguist can think it in their turn; it is all right also to say that these rules should allow us to realize what is said or thought by these individuals. But to say that these regularities are connected, as conditions of existence, to the human mind or its nature is difficult for me to accept: it seems to me that one must, before reaching that point—and in any case I am talking only about the understanding—replace it in the field of other human practices, such as economics, technology, politics, sociology, which can serve them as conditions of formation, of models, of place, of apparition, etc. I would like to know whether one cannot discover the system of regularity, of constraint, which makes science possible, somewhere else, even outside the human mind, in social forms, in the relations of production, in the class struggles, etc.

For example, the fact that at a certain time madness became an object for scientific study, and an object of knowledge in the West, seems to me to be linked to a particular economic and social situation.

Perhaps the point of difference between Mr. Chomsky and myself is that when he speaks of science he probably thinks of the formal organization of knowledge, whereas I am speaking of knowledge itself, that is to say, I think of the content of various knowledges which is dispersed into a particular society, permeates through that society, and asserts itself as the foundation for education, for theories, for practices, etc.

ELDERS: But what does this theory of knowledge mean for your theme of the death of man or the end of the period of the nineteenth to twentieth centuries?

FOUCAULT: But this doesn't have any relation to what we are talking about.

ELDERS: I don't know, because I was trying to apply what you have said to your anthropological notion. You have already refused to speak about your own creativity and freedom, haven't you? Well, I'm wondering what are the psychological reasons for this . . .

FOUCAULT: [*Protesting.*] Well, you can wonder about it, but I can't help that.

ELDERS: But what are the objective reasons, in relation to your conception of understanding, of knowledge, of science, for refusing to answer these personal questions?

When there is a problem for you to answer, what are your reasons for making a problem out of a personal question?

FOUCAULT: No, I'm not making a problem out of a personal question, I make of a personal question an absence of a problem.

Let me take a very simple example, which I will not analyze, but which is this: How was it possible that men began, at the end of the eighteenth century, for the first time in the history of Western thought and of Western knowledge, to open up the corpses of people in order to know what was the source, the origin, the anatomical needle, of the particular malady which was responsible for their deaths?

The idea seems simple enough. Well, four or five thousand years of medicine in the West were needed before we had the idea of looking for the cause of the malady in the lesion of a corpse.

If you tried to explain this by the personality of Bichat, I believe that would be without interest. If, on the contrary, you tried to establish the place of disease and of death in society at the end of the eighteenth century, and what interest industrial society effectively had in quadrupling the entire population in order to expand and develop itself, as a result of which medical surveys of society were made, big hospitals were opened, etc.; if you tried to find out how medical knowledge became institutionalized in that period, how its relations with other kinds of knowledge were ordered, well, then you could see how the relationship between disease, the hospitalized ill person, the corpse, and pathological anatomy were made possible.

Here is, I believe, a form of analysis which I don't say is new, but which in any case has been much too neglected; and personal events have almost nothing to do with it.

ELDERS: Yes, but nevertheless it would have been very interesting for us to know a little bit more about your arguments to refute this.

Could you, Mr. Chomsky—and as far as I'm concerned, it's my last question about this philosophical part of the debate—

give your ideas about, for example, the way the social sciences are working? I'm thinking here especially about your severe attacks on behaviorism. And perhaps you could even explain a little the way Mr. Foucault is now working in a more or less behavioristic way. [*Both philosophers laugh.*]

CHOMSKY: I would like to depart from your injunction very briefly, just to make one comment about what Mr. Foucault just said.

I think that illustrates very nicely the way in which we're digging into the mountain from opposite directions, to use your original image. That is, I think that an act of scientific creation depends on two facts: one, some intrinsic property of the mind, another, some set of social and intellectual conditions that exist. And it is not a question, as I see it, of which of these we should study; rather we will understand scientific discovery, and similarly any other kind of discovery, when we know what these factors are and can therefore explain how they interact in a particular fashion.

My particular interest, in this connection at least, is with the intrinsic capacities of the mind; yours, as you say, is in the particular arrangement of social and economic and other conditions.

FOUCAULT: But I don't believe that difference is connected to our characters. It's connected to the state of knowledge, of knowing, in which we are working. The linguistics with which you have been familiar, and which you have succeeded in transforming, excluded the importance of the creative subject, of the creative speaking subject; while the history of science such as it existed when people of my generation were starting to work, on the contrary, exalted individual creativity and put aside these collective rules.

AUDIENCE: It goes a bit back in your discussion, but what I should like to know, Mr. Chomsky, is this: you suppose a basic system of what must be in a way elementary limitations that are present in what you call human nature; to what extent do you think these are subject to historical change? Do you think, for instance, that they have changed substantially since, let's say, the seventeenth century? In that case, you could perhaps connect this with the ideas of Mr. Foucalt?

CHOMSKY: Well, I think that as a matter of biological and anthropological fact, the nature of human intelligence certainly has not changed in any substantial way, at least since the seventeenth century, or probably since Cro-Magnon man. That is, I think that the fundamental properties of our intelligence, those that are within the domain of what we are discussing tonight, are certainly very ancient; and that if you took a man from five thousand or maybe twenty thousand years ago and placed him as a child within today's society, he would learn what everyone else learns, and he would be a genius or a fool or something else, but he wouldn't be fundamentally different.

But, of course, the level of acquired knowledge changes, social conditions change—those conditions that permit a person to think freely and break through the bonds of, let's say, superstitious constraint. And as those conditions change, a given human intelligence will progress to new forms of creation. In fact this relates very closely to the last question that Mr. Elders put, if I can perhaps say a word about that.

Take behavioral science, and think of it in these contexts. It seems to me that the fundamental property of behaviorism, which is in a way suggested by the odd term *behavioral science*, is that it is a negation of the possibility of developing a scientific theory. That is, what defines behaviorism is the very curious and self-destructive assumption that you are *not* permitted to create an interesting theory.

If physics, for example, had made the assumption that you have to keep to phenomena and their arrangement and such things, we would be doing Babylonian astronomy today. Fortunately physicists never made this ridiculous, extraneous assumption, which has its own historical reasons and had to do with all sorts of curious facts about the historical context in which behaviorism evolved.

But looking at it purely intellectually, behaviorism is the arbitrary insistence that one must not create a scientific theory of human behavior; rather one must deal directly with phenomena and their interrelation, and no more—something which is totally impossible in any other domain, and I assume impossible in the domain of human intelligence or human behavior as well. So in this sense I don't think that behaviorism is a science. Here is a case in point of just the kind of thing that you mentioned and that Mr. Foucault is discussing: under certain historical circumstances, for example those in which experimental psychology developed, it was—for some reason which I won't go into—interesting and maybe important to impose some very strange limitations on the kind of scientific theory construction that was permitted, and those very strange limitations are known as behaviorism. Well, it has long since run its course, I think. Whatever value it may have had in 1880, it has no function today except constraining and limiting scientific inquiry and should therefore simply be dispensed with, in the same way one would dispense with a physicist who said: you're not allowed to develop a general physical theory, you're only allowed to plot the motions of the planets and make up more epicycles and so on and so forth. One forgets about that and puts it aside. Similarly one should put aside the very curious restrictions that define behaviorism; restrictions which are, as I said before, very much suggested by the term *behavioral science* itself.

We can agree, perhaps, that behavior in some broad sense constitutes the data for the science of man. But to define a science by its data would be to define physics as the theory of meter-readings. And if a physicist were to say: yes, I'm involved in meter-reading science, we could be pretty sure that he was not going to get very far. They might talk about meter-readings and correlations between them and such things, but they wouldn't ever create physical theory.

And so the term itself is symptomatic of the disease in this case. We should understand the historical context in which these curious limitations developed, and having understood them, I believe, discard them and proceed in the science of man as we would in any other domain, that is by discarding entirely behaviorism and in fact, in my view, the entire empiricist tradition from which it evolved.

AUDIENCE: So you are not willing to link your theory about innate limitations with Mr. Foucault's theory of the "grille." There might be a certain connection. You see, Mr. Foucault says that an upsurge of creativity in a certain direction automatically removes knowledge in another direction, by a system of "grilles." Well, if you had a changing system of limitations, this might be connected.

CHOMSKY: Well, the reason for what he describes, I think, is different. Again, I'm oversimplifying. We have more possible sciences available intellectually. When we try out those intellectual constructions in a changing world of fact, we will not find cumulative growth. What we will find are strange leaps: here is a domain of phenomena, a certain science applies very nicely; now slightly broaden the range of phenomena, then another science, which is very different, happens to apply very beautifully, perhaps leaving out some of these other phenomena. Okay, that's scientific progress, and that leads to the omission or forgetting of certain domains. But I think the reason for this is precisely this set of principles, which unfortunately, we don't know, which makes the whole discussion rather abstract, which defines for us what is a possible intellectual structure, a possible deep-science, if you like.

ELDERS: Well, let's move over now to the second part of the discussion, to politics. First of all I would like to ask Mr. Foucault why he is so interested in politics, because he told me that in fact he likes politics much more than philosophy.

FOUCAULT: I've never concerned myself, in any case, with philosophy. But that is not a problem. [*He laughs.*]

Your question is: why am I so interested in politics? But if I were to answer you very simply, I would say this: why *shouldn't* I be interested? That is to say, what blindness, what deafness,

what density of ideology would have to weigh me down to prevent me from being interested in what is probably the most
crucial subject to our existence, that is to say the society in
which we live, the economic relations within which it functions,
and the system of power which defines the regular forms and
the regular permissions and prohibitions of our conduct. The
essence of our life consists, after all, of the political functioning
of the society in which we find ourselves.

So I can't answer the question of why I should be interested; I could only answer it by asking why shouldn't I be
interested? Not to be interested in politics, that's what constitutes a problem. So instead of asking me, you should ask someone who is not interested in politics and then your question
would be well-founded, and you would have the right to say,
"Why, damn it, are you not interested?" [*They laugh and the audience laughs.*]

ELDERS: Well, yes, perhaps. Mr. Chomsky, we are all very interested to know your political objectives, especially in relation to
your well-known anarcho-syndicalism or, as you formulated it,
libertarian socialism. What are the most important goals of
your libertarian socialism?

CHOMSKY: I'll overcome to urge to answer the earlier very interesting question that you asked me and turn to this one.

Let me begin by referring to something that we have already discussed, that is, *if* it is correct, as I believe it is, that a
fundamental element of human nature is the need for creative
work, for creative inquiry, for free creation without the arbitrary limiting effect of coercive institutions, then, of course, it

will follow that a decent society should maximize the possibilities for this fundamental human characteristic to be realized. That means trying to overcome the elements of repression and oppression and destruction and coercion that exist in any existing society, ours for example, as a historical residue.

Now any form of coercion or repression, any form of autocratic control of some domain of existence, let's say, private ownership of capital or state control of some aspects of human life, any such autocratic restriction on some area of human endeavour, can be justified, *if at all, only* in terms of the need for subsistence, or the need for survival, or the need for defense against some horrible fate or something of that sort. It cannot be justified intrinsically. Rather it must be overcome and eliminated.

And I think that, at least in the technologically advanced societies of the West, we are now certainly in a position where meaningless drudgery can very largely be eliminated, and to the marginal extent that it's necessary, can be shared among the population; where centralized autocratic control of, in the first place, economic institutions, by which I mean either private capitalism or state totalitarianism or the various mixed forms of state capitalism that exist here and there, has become a destructive vestige of history.

They are all vestiges that have to be overthrown, eliminated in favor of direct participation in the form of workers' councils or other free associations that individuals will constitute themselves for the purpose of their social existence and their productive labor.

Now a federated, decentralized system of free associations, incorporating economic as well as other social institutions, would be what I refer to as anarcho-syndicalism; and it seems to me that this is the appropriate form of social organization for an advanced technological society, in which human beings do *not* have to be forced into the position of tools, of cogs in the machine. There is no longer any social necessity for human beings to be treated as mechanical elements in the productive process; that can be overcome and we must overcome it by a society of freedom and free association, in which the creative urge that I consider intrinsic to human nature will in fact be able to realize itself in whatever way it will.

And again, like Mr. Foucault, I don't see how any human being can fail to be interested in this question. [*Foucault laughs.*]

ELDERS: Do you believe, Mr. Foucault, that we can call our societies in any way democratic, after listening to this statement from Mr. Chomsky?

FOUCAULT: No, I don't have the least belief that one could consider our society democratic. [*Laughs.*]

If one understands by democracy the effective exercise of power by a population which is neither divided nor hierarchically ordered in classes, it is quite clear that we are very far from democracy. It is only too clear that we are living under a regime of a dictatorship of class, of a power of class which imposes itself by violence, even when the instruments of this violence are institutional and constitutional; and to that degree, there isn't any question of democracy for us.

Well. When you asked me why I was interested in politics, I refused to answer because it seemed evident to me, but perhaps your question was, How am I interested in it?

And had you asked me that question, and in a certain sense

I could say you have, I would say to you that I am much less advanced in my way, I go much less far than Mr. Chomsky. That is to say that I admit to not being able to define, nor for even stronger reasons to propose, an ideal social model for the functioning of our scientific or technological society.

On the other hand, one of the tasks that seems immediate and urgent to me, over and above anything else, is this: that we should indicate and show up, even where they are hidden, all the relationships of political power which actually control the social body and oppress or repress it.

What I want to say is this: it is the custom, at least in European society, to consider that power is localized in the hands of the government and that it is exercised through a certain number of particular institutions, such as the administration, the police, the army, and the apparatus of the state. One knows that all these institutions are made to elaborate and to transmit a certain number of decisions, in the name of the nation or of the state, to have them applied and to punish those who don't obey. But I believe that political power also exercises itself through the mediation of a certain number of institutions which look as if they have nothing in common with the political power, and as if they are independent of it, while they are not.

One knows this in relation to the family; and one knows that the university, and in a general way, all teaching systems, which appear simply to disseminate knowledge, are made to maintain a certain social class in power; and to exclude the instruments of power of another social class. Institutions of knowledge, of foresight and care, such as medicine, also help to support the political power. It's also obvious, even to the point of scandal, in certain cases related to psychiatry.

It seems to me that the real political task in a society such as ours is to criticize the workings of institutions, which appear to be both neutral and independent; to criticize and attack them in such a manner that the political violence which has always exercised itself obscurely through them will be unmasked, so that one can fight against them.

This critique and this fight seem essential to me for different reasons: first, because political power goes much deeper than one suspects; there are centers and invisible, little-known points of support; its true resistance, its true solidity is perhaps where one doesn't expect it. Probably it's insufficient to say that behind the governments, behind the apparatus of the state, there is the dominant class; one must locate the point of activity, the places and forms in which its domination is exercised. And because this domination is not simply the expression in political terms of economic exploitation, it is its instrument and, to a large extent, the condition which makes it possible; the suppression of the one is achieved through the exhaustive discernment of the other. Well, if one fails to recognize these points of support of class power, one risks allowing them to continue to exist; and to see this class power reconstitute itself even after an apparent revolutionary process.

CHOMSKY: Yes, I would certainly agree with that, not only in theory but also in action. That is, there are two intellectual tasks: one, and the one that I was discussing, is to try to create the vision of a future just society; that is to create, if you like, a humanistic social theory that is based, if possible, on some firm and humane concept of the human essence or human nature. That's one task.

Another task is to understand very clearly the nature of power and oppression and terror and destruction in our own society. And that certainly includes the institutions you mentioned, as well as the central institutions of any industrial society, namely the economic, commercial and financial institutions and in particular, in the coming period, the great multi-national corporations, which are not very far from us physically tonight [i.e., Philips at Eindhoven].

Those are the basic institutions of oppression and coercion and autocratic rule that appear to be neutral despite everything they say: well, we're subject to the democracy of the marketplace, and that must be understood precisely in terms of their autocratic power, including the particular form of autocratic control that comes from the domination of market forces in an inegalitarian society.

Surely we must understand these facts, and not only understand them but combat them. And in fact, as far as one's own political involvements are concerned, in which one spends the majority of one's energy and effort, it seems to me that they must certainly be in that area. I don't want to get personal about it, but my own certainly are in that area, and I assume everyone's are.

Still, I think it would be a great shame to put aside entirely the somewhat more abstract and philosophical task of trying to draw the connections between a concept of human nature that gives full scope to freedom and dignity and creativity and other fundamental human characteristics, and to relate that to some notion of social structure in which those properties could be realized and in which meaningful human life could take place.

And in fact, if we are thinking of social transformation or

social revolution, though it would be absurd, of course, to try to sketch out in detail the goal that we are hoping to reach, still we should know something about where we think we are going, and such a theory may tell it to us.

FOUCAULT: Yes, but then isn't there a danger here? If you say that a certain human nature exists, that this human nature has not been given in actual society the rights and the possibilities which allow it to realize itself . . . that's really what you have said, I believe.

CHOMSKY: Yes.

FOUCAULT: And if one admits that, doesn't one risk defining this human nature—which is at the same time ideal and real, and has been hidden and repressed until now—in terms borrowed from our society, from our civilization, from our culture?

I will take an example by greatly simplifying it. The socialism of a certain period, at the end of the nineteenth century and the beginning of the twentieth century, admitted in effect that in capitalist societies man hadn't realized the full potential for his development and self-realization; that human nature was effectively alienated in the capitalist system. And it dreamed of an ultimately liberated human nature.

What model did it use to conceive, project, and eventually realize that human nature? It was in fact the bourgeois model.

It considered that an alienated society was a society which, for example, gave pride of place to the benefit of all, to a sexuality of a bourgeois type, to a family of a bourgeois type, to an aesthetic of a bourgeois type. And it is moreover very true that this has happened in the Soviet Union and in the popular democracies: a kind of society has been reconstituted which has been transposed from the bourgeois society of the nineteenth century. The universalization of the model of the bourgeois has been the utopia which has animated the constitution of Soviet society.

The result is that you, too, realized, I think, that it is difficult to say exactly what human nature is.

Isn't there a risk that we will be led into error? Mao Tse-Tung spoke of bourgeois human nature and proletarian human nature, and he considers that they are not the same thing.

CHOMSKY: Well, you see, I think that in the intellectual domain of political action, that is the domain of trying to construct a vision of a just and free society on the basis of some notion of human nature, we face the very same problem that we face in immediate political action, namely, that of being impelled to do something, because the problems are so great, and yet knowing that whatever we do is on the basis of a very partial understanding of the social realities, and the human realities in this case.

For example, to be quite concrete, a lot of my own activity really has to do with the Vietnam War, and some of my own energy goes into civil disobedience. Well, civil disobedience in the U.S. is an action undertaken in the face of considerable uncertainties about its effects. For example, it threatens the social order in ways which might, one might argue, bring about fascism; and that would be a very bad thing for America, for Vietnam, for Holland, and for everyone else. You know, if a great Leviathan like the United States were really to become fascist, a lot of problems would result; so that is one danger in undertaking this concrete act.

On the other hand there is a great danger in not undertaking it, namely, if you don't undertake it, the society of Indochina will be torn to shreds by American power. In the face of these uncertainties one has to choose a course of action.

Well, similarly in the intellectual domain, one is faced with the uncertainties that you correctly pose. Our concept of human nature is certainly limited; it's partially socially conditioned, constrained by our own character defects and the limitations of the intellectual culture in which we exist. Yet at the same time it is of critical importance that we know what impossible goals we're trying to achieve, if we hope to achieve some of the possible goals. And that means that we have to be bold enough to speculate and create social theories on the basis of partial knowledge, while remaining very open to the strong possibility, and in fact overwhelming probability, that at least in some respects we're very far off the mark.

ELDERS: Well, perhaps it would be interesting to delve a little deeper into this problem of strategy. I suppose that what you call civil disobedience is probably the same as what we call extra-parliamentary action?

CHOMSKY: No, I think it goes beyond that.

Extra-parliamentary action would include, let's say, a mass legal demonstration, but civil disobedience is narrower than all extra-parliamentary action, in that it means direct defiance of what is alleged, incorrectly in my view, by the state to be law.

ELDERS: So, for example, in the case of Holland, we had something like a population census. One was obliged to answer questions on official forms. You would call it civil disobedience if one refused to fill in the forms?

CHOMSKY: Right. I would be a little bit careful about that, because, going back to a very important point that Mr. Foucault made, one does not necessarily allow the state to define what is legal. Now the state has the power to enforce a certain concept of what is legal, but power doesn't imply justice or even correctness; so that the state may define something as civil disobedience and may be wrong in doing so.

For example, in the United States the state defines it as civil disobedience to, let's say, derail an ammunition train that's going to Vietnam; and the state is *wrong* in defining that as civil disobedience, because it's legal and proper and should be done. It's proper to carry out actions that will prevent the criminal acts of the state, just as it is proper to violate a traffic ordinance in order to prevent a murder.

If I had stopped my car in front of a traffic light which was red, and then I drove through the red traffic light to prevent somebody from, let's say, machine-gunning a group of people, of course that's not an illegal act, it's an appropriate and proper action; no sane judge would convict you for such an action.

Similarly, a good deal of what the state authorities define as civil disobedience is not really civil disobedience: in fact, it's legal, obligatory behavior in violation of the commands of the state, which may or may not be legal commands.

So one has to be rather careful about calling things illegal, I think.

FOUCAULT: Yes, but I would like to ask you a question. When, in the United States, you commit an illegal act, do you justify it in terms of justice or of a superior legality, or do you justify it by the necessity of the class struggle, which is at the present time essential for the proletariat in their struggle against the ruling class?

CHOMSKY: Well, here I would like to take the point of view which is taken by the American Supreme Court and probably other courts in such circumstances; that is, to try to settle the issue on the narrowest possible grounds. I would think that ultimately it would make very good sense, in many cases, to act against the legal institutions of a given society, if in so doing you're striking at the sources of power and oppression in that society.

However, to a very large extent existing law represents certain human values, which are decent human values: and existing law, correctly interpreted, permits much of what the state commands you not to do. And I think it's important to exploit the areas of law which are properly formulated and then perhaps to act directly against those areas of law which simply ratify some system of power.

FOUCAULT: My question, my question was this: when you commit a clearly illegal act . . .

CHOMSKY: . . . which *I* regard as illegal, not just the state.

FOUCAULT: No, no, well, the state's . . .

CHOMSKY: . . . that the state regards as illegal . . .

FOUCAULT: . . . that the state considers as illegal. Are you committing this act in virtue of an ideal justice, or because the class struggle makes it useful and necessary? Do you refer to ideal justice, that's my problem.

CHOMSKY: Again, very often when I do something which the state regards as illegal, I regard it as legal: that is, I regard the state as criminal. But in some instances that's not true. Let me be quite concrete about it and move from the area of class war to imperialist war, where the situation is somewhat clearer and easier.

Take international law, a very weak instrument as we know, but nevertheless one that incorporates some very interesting principles. Well, international law is, in many respects, the instrument of the powerful: it is a creation of states and their representatives. In developing the presently existing body of international law, there was no participation by mass movements of peasants.

The structure of international law reflects that fact; that is, international law permits much too wide a range of forceful intervention in support of existing power structures that define themselves as states against the interests of masses of people who happen to be organized in opposition to states.

Now that's a fundamental defect of international law and I think one is justified in opposing that aspect of international law as having no validity, as having no more validity than the divine right of kings. It's simply an instrument of the powerful to retain their power.

But, in fact, international law is not *solely* of that kind. And in fact there are interesting elements of international law, for example, embedded in the Nuremberg principles and the United Nations Charter, which permit, in fact, I believe, *require* the citizen to act against his own state in ways which the state will falsely regard as criminal. Nevertheless, he's acting legally, because international law also happens to prohibit the threat or use of force in international affairs, except under some very narrow circumstances, of which, for example, the war in Vietnam is not one. This means that in the particular case of the Vietnam War, which interests me most, the American state is acting in a criminal capacity. And the people have the right to stop criminals from committing murder. Just because the criminal happens to call your action illegal when you try to stop him, it doesn't mean it *is* illegal.

A perfectly clear case of that is the present case of the Pentagon Papers in the United States, which, I suppose, you know about.

Reduced to its essentials and forgetting legalisms, what is happening is that the state is trying to prosecute people for exposing its crimes. That's what it amounts to.

Now, obviously that's absurd, and one must pay no attention whatsoever to that distortion of any reasonable judicial process. Furthermore, I think that the existing system of law even explains *why* it is absurd. But if it didn't, we would then have to oppose that system of law.

FOUCAULT: So it is in the name of a purer justice that you criticize the functioning of justice?

There is an important question for us here. It is true that in all social struggles, there is a question of "justice." To put it more precisely, the fight against class justice, against its injustice, is always part of the social struggle: to dismiss the judges, to change the tribunals, to amnesty the condemned, to open the prisons, has always been part of social transformations as soon as they become slightly violent. At the present time in France the function of justice and the police is the target of many attacks from those whom we call the "gauchistes." But if justice is at stake in a struggle, then it is as an instrument of power; it is not in the hope that finally one day, in this or another society, people will be rewarded according to their merits, or punished according to their faults. Rather than thinking of the social struggle in terms of "justice," one has to emphasize justice in terms of the social struggle.

CHOMSKY: Yeah, but surely you believe that your role in the war is a just role, that you are fighting a just war, to bring in a concept from another domain. And that, I think, is important. If you thought that you were fighting an unjust war, you couldn't follow that line of reasoning.

I would like to slightly reformulate what you said. It seems to me that the difference isn't between legality and ideal justice; it's rather between legality and better justice.

I would agree that we are certainly in no position to create a system of ideal justice, just as we are in no position to create an ideal society in our minds. We don't know enough and we're too limited and too biased and all sorts of other things. But we are in a position—and we must act as sensitive and responsible human beings in that position—to imagine and move towards the creation of a better society and also a better system of justice. Now this better system will certainly have its defects. But if one compares the better system with the existing system, without being confused into thinking that our better system is the ideal system, we can then argue, I think, as follows:

The concept of legality and the concept of justice are not identical; they're not entirely distinct either. Insofar as legality incorporates justice in this sense of better justice, referring to a better society, then we should follow and obey the law, and force the state to obey the law, and force the great corporations to obey the law, and force the police to obey the law, if we have the power to do so.

Of course, in those areas where the legal system happens to represent not better justice, but rather the techniques of oppression that have been codified in a particular autocratic system, well, then a reasonable human being should disregard and oppose them, at least in principle; he may not, for some reason, do it in fact.

FOUCAULT: But I would merely like to reply to your first sentence, in which you said that if you didn't consider the war you make against the police to be just, you wouldn't make it.

I would like to reply to you in terms of Spinoza and say that the proletariat doesn't wage war against the ruling class because it considers such a war to be just. The proletariat makes war with the ruling class because, for the first time in history, it wants to take power. And because it will overthrow the power of the ruling class, it considers such a war to be just.

CHOMSKY: Yeah, I don't agree.

FOUCAULT: One makes war to win, not because it is just.

CHOMSKY: I don't, personally, agree with that.

For example, if I could convince myself that attainment of

power by the proletariat would lead to a terrorist police state, in which freedom and dignity and decent human relations would be destroyed, then I wouldn't want the proletariat to take power. In fact the only reason for wanting any such thing, I believe, is because one thinks, rightly or wrongly, that some fundamental human values will be achieved by that transfer of power.

FOUCAULT: When the proletariat takes power, it may be quite possible that the proletariat will exert towards the classes over which it has just triumphed, a violent, dictatorial, and even bloody power. I can't see what objection one could make to this.

But if you ask me what would be the case if the proletariat exerted bloody, tyrannical, and unjust power towards itself, then I would say that this could only occur if the proletariat hadn't really taken power, but that a class outside the proletariat, a group of people inside the proletariat, a bureaucracy, or petit bourgeois elements had taken power.

CHOMSKY: Well, I'm not at all satisfied with that theory of revolution for a lot of reasons, historical and others. But even if one were to accept it for the sake of argument, still that theory maintains that it is proper for the proletariat to take power and exercise it in a violent and bloody and unjust fashion, because it is claimed, and in my opinion falsely, that that will lead to a more just society, in which the state will wither away, in which the proletariat will be a universal class, and so on and so forth. If it weren't for that future justification, the concept of a violent and bloody dictatorship of the proletariat would certainly be unjust. Now this is another issue, but I'm very sceptical about the idea of a violent and bloody dictatorship of the proletariat, especially when expressed by self-appointed representatives of a vanguard party, who, we have enough historical experience to know and might have predicted in advance, will simply be the new rulers over this society.

FOUCAULT: Yes, but I haven't been talking about the power of the proletariat, which in itself would be an unjust power; you are right in saying that this would obviously be too easy. I would like to say that the power of the proletariat could, in a certain period, imply violence and a prolonged war against a social class over which its triumph or victory was not yet totally assured.

CHOMSKY: Well, look, I'm not saying there is an absolute. . . . For example, I am not a committed pacifist. I would not hold that it is under all imaginable circumstances wrong to use violence, even though use of violence is in some sense unjust. I believe that one has to estimate relative justices.

But the use of violence and the creation of some degree of injustice can only be justified on the basis of the claim and the assessment—which always ought to be undertaken very, very seriously and with a good deal of skepticism—that this violence is being exercised because a more just result is going to be achieved. If it does not have such a grounding, it is really totally immoral, in my opinion.

FOUCAULT: I don't think that as far as the aim which the proletariat proposes for itself in leading a class struggle is concerned, it would be sufficient to say that it is in itself a greater justice. What the proletariat will achieve by expelling the class which is at present in power and by taking over power itself, is precisely the suppression of the power of class in general.

CHOMSKY: Okay, but that's the further justification.

FOUCAULT: That is the justification, but one doesn't speak in terms of justice but in terms of power.

CHOMSKY: But it *is* in terms of justice; it's because the end that will be achieved is claimed as a just one.

No Leninist or whatever you like would dare to say, "We, the proletariat, have a right to take power, and then throw everyone else into crematoria." If that were the consequence of the proletariat taking power, of course it would not be appropriate.

The idea is—and for the reasons I mentioned I'm sceptical about it—that a period of violent dictatorship, or perhaps violent and bloody dictatorship, is justified because it will mean the submergence and termination of class oppression, a proper end to achieve in human life; it is because of that final qualification that the whole enterprise might be justified. Whether it is or not is another issue.

FOUCAULT: If you like, I will be a little bit Nietzschean about this; in other words, it seems to me that the idea of justice in itself is an idea which in effect has been invented and put to work in different types of societies as an instrument of a certain political and economic power or as a weapon against that power. But it seems to me that, in any case, the notion of justice itself functions within a society of classes as a claim made by the oppressed class and as justification for it.

CHOMSKY: I don't agree with that.

FOUCAULT: And in a classless society, I am not sure that we would still use this notion of justice.

CHOMSKY: Well, here I really disagree. I think there is some sort of an absolute basis—if you press me too hard I'll be in trouble, because I can't sketch it out—ultimately residing in fundamental human qualities, in terms of which a "real" notion of justice is grounded.

I think it's too hasty to characterize our existing systems of justice as merely systems of class oppression; I don't think that they are that. I think that they embody systems of class oppression and elements of other kinds of oppression, but they also embody a kind of groping towards the true humanly valuable concepts of justice and decency and love and kindness and sympathy, which I think are real.

And I think that in any future society, which will, of course, never be the perfect society, we'll have such concepts again, which we hope, will come closer to incorporating a defense of fundamental human needs, including such needs as those for solidarity and sympathy and whatever, but will probably still reflect in some manner the inequities and the elements of oppression of the existing society.

However, I think what you're describing only holds for a very different kind of situation.

For example, let's take a case of national conflict. Here are two societies, each trying to destroy the other. No question of justice arises. The only question that arises is, Which side are you on? Are you going to defend your own society and destroy the other?

I mean, in a certain sense, abstracting away from a lot of historical problems, that's what faced the soldiers who were massacring each other in the trenches in the First World War. They were fighting for nothing. They were fighting for the right to destroy each other. And in that kind of circumstance no questions of justice arise.

And of course there were rational people, most of them in jail, like Karl Liebknecht, for example, who pointed that out and were in jail because they did so, or Bertrand Russell, to take another example on the other side. There were people who understood that there was no point to that mutual massacre in terms of any sort of justice and that they ought to just call it off.

Now those people were regarded as madmen or lunatics and criminals or whatever, but of course they were the only sane people around.

And in such a circumstance, the kind that you describe, where there is no question of justice, just the question of who's going to win a struggle to the death, then I think the proper human reaction is: call it off, don't win either way, try to stop it—and of course if you say that, you'll immediately be thrown in jail or killed or something of that sort, the fate of a lot of rational people.

But I don't think that's the typical situation in human affairs, and I don't think that's the situation in the case of class conflict or social revolution. There I think that one can and *must* give an argument, if you can't give an argument you should extract yourself from the struggle. Give an argument that the social revolution that you're trying to achieve *is* in the ends of justice, *is* in the ends of realizing fundamental human needs, not merely in the ends of putting some other group into power, because they want it.

FOUCAULT: Well, do I have time to answer?

ELDERS: Yes.

FOUCAULT: How much? Because . . .

ELDERS: Two minutes. [*Foucault laughs.*]

FOUCAULT: But I would say that that is unjust. [*Everybody laughs.*]

CHOMSKY: Absolutely, yes.

FOUCAULT: No, but I don't want to answer in so little time. I would simply say this, that finally this problem of human nature, when put simply in theoretical terms, hasn't led to an argument between us; ultimately we understand each other very well on these theoretical problems.

On the other hand, when we discussed the problem of human nature and political problems, then differences arose between us. And contrary to what you think, you can't prevent me from believing that these notions of human nature, of justice, of the realization of the essence of human beings, are all notions and concepts which have been formed within our civilization, within our type of knowledge and our form of philosophy, and that as a result form part of our class system; and one can't, however regrettable it may be, put forward these notions to describe or justify a fight which should—and shall in principle— overthrow the very fundaments of our society. This is an extrapolation for which I can't find the historical justification. That's the point . . .

CHOMSKY: It's clear.

ELDERS: Mr. Foucault, if you were obliged to describe our actual society in pathological terms, which of its kinds of madness would most impress you?

FOUCAULT: In our contemporary society?

ELDERS: Yes.

FOUCAULT: If I were to say with which malady contemporary society is most afflicted?

ELDERS: Yes.

FOUCAULT: The definition of disease and of the insane, and the classification of the insane have been made in such a way as to exclude from our society a certain number of people. If our society characterized itself as insane, it would exclude itself. It pretends to do so for reasons of internal reform. Nobody is more conservative than those people who tell you that the modern world is afflicted by nervous anxiety or schizophrenia. It is in fact a cunning way of excluding certain people or certain patterns of behavior.

So I don't think that one can, except as a metaphor or a game, validly say that our society is schizophrenic or paranoid, unless one gives these words a non-psychiatric meaning. But if you were to push me to an extreme, I would say that our society has been afflicted by a disease, a very curious, a very paradoxical disease, for which we haven't yet found a name; and this mental disease has a very curious symptom, which is that the symptom itself brought the mental disease into being. There you have it.

ELDERS: Great. Well, I think we can immediately start the discussion.

AUDIENCE: Mr. Chomsky, I would like to ask you one question. In your discussion you used the term *proletariat*; what do you mean by *proletariat* in a highly developed technological society? I think this is a Marxist notion, which doesn't represent the exact sociological state of affairs.

CHOMSKY: Yes, I think you are right, and that is one of the reasons why I kept hedging on that issue and saying I'm very skeptical about the whole idea, because I think the notion of a proletariat, if we want to use it, has to be given a new interpretation fitting to our present social conditions. Really, I'd even like to drop the word, since it's so loaded with specific historical connotations, and think instead of the people who do the productive work of the society, manual and intellectual work. I think those people should be in a position to organize the conditions of their work, and to determine the ends of their work and the uses to which it's put; and, because of my concept of human nature, I really think of that as partially including everyone. Because I think that any human being who is not physically or mentally deformed—and here I again must disagree with Monsieur Foucault and express my belief that the concept of mental illness probably *does* have an absolute character, to some extent at least—is not only capable of, but is insistent upon doing productive, creative work, if given the opportunity to do so.

I've never seen a child who didn't want to build something out of blocks, or learn something new, or try the next task. And the only reason why adults aren't like that is, I suppose, that they have been sent to school and other oppressive institutions, which have driven that out of them.

Now if that's the case, then the proletariat, or whatever you want to call it, can really be universal, that is, it can be all those human beings who are impelled by what I believe to be the fundamental human need to be yourself, which means to be creative, to be exploratory, to be inquisitive, to do useful things, you know.

AUDIENCE: If you use such a category, which has another meaning in Marxist . . .

CHOMSKY: That's why I say maybe we ought to drop the concept.

AUDIENCE: Wouldn't you do better to use another term? In this situation I would like to ask another question: which groups, do you think, will make the revolution? It's an irony of history that at this moment young intellectuals, coming from the middle and upper classes, call themselves proletarians and say we must join the proletarians. But I don't see any class-conscious proletarians. And that the great dilemma.

CHOMSKY: Okay. Now I think you're asking a concrete and specific question, and a very reasonable one.

It is not true in our given society that all people are doing useful, productive work, or self-satisfying work—obviously that's very far from true—or that, if they were to do the kind of work they're doing under conditions of freedom, it would thereby become productive and satisfying.

Rather there are a very large number of people who are involved in other kinds of work. For example, the people who are involved in the management of exploitation, or the people who are involved in the creation of artificial consumption, or the people who are involved in the creation of mechanisms of destruction and oppression, or the people who are simply not given any place in a stagnating industrial economy. Lots of people are excluded from the possibility of productive labor.

And I think that the revolution, if you like, should be in the *name* of all human beings; but it will have to be conducted by certain categories of human beings, and those will be, I think, the human beings who really *are* involved in the productive work of society. Now *what* this is will differ, depending upon the society. In our society it includes, I think, intellectual workers; it includes a spectrum of people that runs from manual laborers to skilled workers, to engineers, to scientists, to a very large class of professionals, to many people in the so-called service occupations, which really do constitute the over-whelming mass of the population, at least in the United States, and I suppose probably here too, and will become the mass of the population in the future.

And so I think that the student-revolutionaries, if you like, have a point, a partial point: that is to say, it's a very important thing in a modern advanced industrial society how the trained intelligentsia identifies itself. It's very important to ask whether they are going to identify themselves as social managers, whether they are going to be technocrats, or servants of either the state or private power, or, alternatively, whether they are going to identify themselves as part of the work force, who happen to be doing intellectual labor.

If the latter, then they can and should play a decent role in a progressive social revolution. If the former, then they're part of the class of oppressors.

AUDIENCE: I was struck, Mr. Chomsky, by what you said about the intellectual necessity of creating new models of society. One of the problems we have in doing this with student groups in Utrecht is that we are looking for consistency of values. One of the values you more or less mentioned is the necessity of de-centralization of power. People on the spot should participate in decision-making.

That's the value of decentralization and participation: but on the other hand we're living in a society that makes it more and more necessary—or seems to make it more and more necessary—that decisions are made on a worldwide scale. And in order to have, for example, a more equal distribution of welfare, etc., it might be necessary to have more centralization.

These problems should be solved on a higher level. Well, that's one of the inconsistencies we found in creating your models of society, and we should like to hear some of your ideas on it.

I've one small additional question—or rather a remark—to make to you. That is: how can you, with your very courageous attitude towards the war in Vietnam, survive in an institution like MIT, which is known here as one of the great war contractors and intellectual makers of this war?

CHOMSKY: Well, let me answer the second question first, hoping that I don't forget the first one. Oh, no, I'll try the first question first; and then remind me if I forget the second.

In general, I am in favor of decentralization. I wouldn't want to make it an absolute principle, but the reason I would be in favor of it, even though there certainly is, I think, a wide margin of speculation here, is because I would imagine that in general a system of centralized power will operate very efficiently in the interest of the most powerful elements *within it.*

Now a system of decentralized power and free association will of course face the problem, the specific problem that you mention, of inequity—one region is richer than the other, etc. But my own guess is that we're safer in trusting to what I hope are the fundamental human emotions of sympathy and the search for justice, which may arise within a system of free association.

I think we're safer in hoping for progress on the basis of those human instincts than on the basis of the institutions of centralized power, which, I believe, will almost inevitably act in the interest of their most powerful components.

Now that's a little abstract and too general, and I wouldn't want to claim that it's a rule for all occasions, but I think it's a principle that's effective in a lot of occasions.

So, for example, I think that a democratic socialist libertarian United States would be more likely to give substantial aid to East Pakistani refugees than a system of centralized power which is basically operating in the interest of multi-national corporations. And, you know, I think the same is true in a lot of other cases. But it seems to me that that principle, at least, deserves some thought.

As to the idea, which was perhaps lurking in your question anyway—it's an idea that's often expressed—that there is some technical imperative, some property of advanced technological society that requires centralized power and decision-making—and a lot of people say that, from Robert McNamara on down—as far as I can see it's perfect nonsense; I've never seen any argument in favour of it.

It seems to me that modern technology, like the technology of data-processing, or communication, and so on, has precisely the opposite implications. It implies that relevant information and relevant understanding can be brought to everyone quickly. It doesn't have to be concentrated in the hands of a small group of managers who control all knowledge, all information, and all decision-making. So technology, I think, can be liberating, it has the property of being possibly liberating; it's converted, like everything else, like the system of justice, into an instrument of oppression because of the fact that power is badly distributed. I don't think there is anything in modern technology or modern technological society that leads away from decentralization of power, quite the contrary.

About the second point, there are two aspects to that: one is the question how MIT tolerates me, and the other question is how I tolerate MIT. [*Laughter.*]

Well, as to how MIT tolerates me, here again, I think, one shouldn't be overly schematic. It's true that MIT is a major institution of war-research. But it's also true that it embodies very important libertarian values, which are, I think, quite deeply embedded in American society, fortunately for the world. They're not deeply embedded enough to save the Vietnamese, but they are deeply embedded enough to prevent far worse disasters.

And here, I think, one has to qualify a bit. There is imperial terror and aggression, there is exploitation, there is racism, lots of things like that. But there is also a real concern, coexisting with it, for individual rights of a sort which, for example, are embodied in the Bill of Rights, which is by no means simply an expression of class oppression. It is also an expression of the necessity to defend the individual against state power.

Now these things coexist. It's not that simple, it's not just all bad or all good. And it's the particular balance in which they coexist that makes an institute that produces weapons of war be willing to tolerate, in fact, in many ways even encourage, a person who is involved in civil disobedience against the war.

Now as to how I tolerate MIT, that raises another question.

There are people who argue, and I have never understood the logic of this, that a radical ought to dissociate himself from oppressive institutions. The logic of that argument is that Karl Marx shouldn't have studied in the British Museum which, if anything, was the symbol of the most vicious imperialism in the world, the place where all the treasures an empire had gathered from the rape of the colonies were brought together.

But I think Karl Marx was quite right in studying in the British Museum. He was right in using the resources and in fact the liberal values of the civilization that he was trying to overcome, against it. And I think the same applies in this case.

AUDIENCE: But aren't you afraid that your presence at MIT gives them a clean conscience?

CHOMSKY: I don't see how, really. I mean, I think my presence at MIT serves marginally to help, I don't know how much, to increase student activism against a lot of the things that MIT as an institution does. At least I *hope* that's what it does.

AUDIENCE: I would like to get back to the question of centralization. You said that technology does not contradict decentralization. But the problem is, can technology criticise itself, its influences, and so forth? Don't you think that it might be necessary to have a central organization that could criticize the influence of technology on the whole universe? And I don't see how that could be incorporated in a small technological institution.

CHOMSKY: Well, I have nothing against the interaction of federated free associations; and in that sense centralization, interaction, communication, argument, debate, can take place, and so on and so forth, and criticism, if you like. What I am talking about is the centralization of power.

AUDIENCE: But of course power is needed, for instance to forbid some technological institutions from doing work that will only benefit the corporation.

CHOMSKY: Yeah, but what I'm arguing is this: if we have the choice between trusting in centralized power to make the right decision in that matter, or trusting in free associations of libertarian communities to make that decision, I would rather trust the latter. And the reason is that I think that they can serve to maximize decent human instincts, whereas a system of centralized power will tend in a general way to maximize one of the worst of human instincts, namely the instinct of rapaciousness, of destructiveness, of accumulating power to oneself and destroying others. It's a kind of instinct which does arise and functions in certain historical circumstances, and I think we want to create the kind of society where it is likely to be repressed and replaced by other and more healthy instincts.

AUDIENCE: I hope you are right.

ELDERS: Well, ladies and gentlemen, I think this must be the end of the debate. Mr. Chomsky, Mr. Foucault, I thank you very much for your far-reaching discussion over the philosophical and theoretical, as well as the political questions of the debate, both for myself and also on behalf of the audience, here and at home.

2.

Politics

Noam Chomsky

MITSOU RONAT: Paradoxically, your political writings and your analyses of American imperialist ideology appear to be better known, in France as well as in the United States, than the new discipline which you have created: generative grammar. That poses the question: Do you see a link between your scientific activities—the study of language—and your political activities? For example, in the methods of analysis?

NOAM CHOMSKY: If there is a connection, it is on a rather abstract level. I don't have access to any unusual methods of analysis, and what special knowledge I have concerning language has no immediate bearing on social and political issues. Everything I have written on these topics could have been written by someone else. There is no very direct connection between my political activities, writing and others, and the work bearing on language structure, though in some measure they perhaps derive from certain common assumptions and attitudes with regard to basic aspects of human nature. Critical analysis in the ideological arena seems to me to be a fairly straightforward matter as compared to an approach that requires a degree of conceptual abstraction. For the analysis of ideology, which occupies me very much, a bit of open-mindedness, normal intelligence, and healthy skepticism will generally suffice.

For example, take the question of the role of the intelligentsia in a society like ours. This social class, which includes historians and other scholars, journalists, political commentators, and so on, undertakes to analyze and present some picture of social reality. By virtue of their analyses and interpretations, they serve as mediators between the social facts and the mass of the population: they create the ideological justification for social practice. Look at the work of the specialists in contemporary affairs and compare their interpretation with the events, compare what they say with the world of fact. You will often find great and fairly systematic divergence. Then you can take a further step and try to explain these divergences, taking into account the class position of the intelligentsia.

Such analysis is, I think, of some importance, but the task is not very difficult, and the problems that arise do not seem to me to pose much of an intellectual challenge. With a little industry and application, anyone who is willing to extricate himself from the system of shared ideology and propaganda will readily see through the modes of distortion developed by substantial segments of the intelligentsia. Everybody is capable of doing that. If such analysis is often carried out poorly, that is because, quite commonly, social and political analysis is produced to defend special interests rather than to account for the actual events.

Precisely because of this tendency one must be careful not to give the impression, which in any event is false, that only intellectuals equipped with special training are capable of such analytic work. In fact that is just what the intelligentsia would often like us to think: they pretend to be engaged in an esoteric enterprise, inaccessible to simple people. But that's nonsense. The social sciences generally, and above all the analysis of contemporary affairs, are quite accessible to anyone who wants to take an interest in these matters. The alleged complexity, depth, and obscurity of these questions is part of the illusion propagated by the system of ideological control, which aims to make the issues seem remote from the general population and to persuade them of their incapacity to organize their own affairs or to understand the social world in which they live without the tutelage of intermediaries. For that reason alone one should be careful not to link the analysis of social issues with scientific topics which, for their part, do require special training and techniques, and thus a special intellectual frame of reference, before they can be seriously investigated.

In the analysis of social and political issues it is sufficient to face the facts and to be willing to follow a rational line of argument. Only Cartesian common sense, which is quite evenly distributed, is needed . . . if by that you understand the willingness to look at the facts with an open mind, to put simple assumptions to the test, and to pursue an argument to its conclusion. But beyond that no special esoteric knowledge is required to explore these "depths," which are nonexistent.

RONAT: In fact I'm thinking of the work which has been able to reveal the existence of "rules" of ideology, inaccessible to the consciousness of those caught up in history; for example, the study which Jean Pierre Faye has devoted to the rise of Nazism. This type of work shows that the critique of ideology can attain intellectual profundity.

CHOMSKY: I do not say that it is impossible to create an intellectually interesting theory dealing with ideology and its social bases. That's possible, but it isn't necessary in order to understand, for example, what induces intellectuals often to disguise reality in the service of external power, or to see how it is done in particular cases of immediate importance. To be sure, one can treat all of this as an interesting topic of research. But we must separate two things:

1. Is it possible to present a significant theoretical analysis of this? Answer: Yes, in principle. And this type of work might attain a level at which it would require special training, and form, in principle, part of science.

2. Is such a science necessary to remove the distorting prism imposed by the intelligentsia on social reality? Answer: No. Ordinary skepticism and application are sufficient.

Let us take a concrete example: When an event occurs in the world, the mass media—television, the newspapers—look for someone to explain it. In the United States, at least, they turn to the professionals in social science, basing themselves on the notion, which seems superficially reasonable and in some instances is reasonable within limits, that these experts have a special competence to explain what is happening. Correspondingly, it is very important for the professionals to make everyone believe in the existence of an intellectual frame of reference which they alone possess, so that they alone have the right to comment on these affairs or are in a position to do so. This is one of the ways in which the professional intelligentsia serve a useful and effective function within the apparatus of social control. You don't ask the man in the street how to build a bridge, do you? You turn to a professional expert. Very well, in the same way you should not ask this man in the street: Must we intervene in Angola? Here one needs professionals—very carefully selected, to be sure.

To make all of this more concrete, let me comment in a very personal way: in my own professional work I have touched on a variety of different fields. I've done work in mathematical linguistics, for example, without any professional credentials in mathematics; in this subject I am completely self-taught, and not very well taught. But I've often been invited by universities to speak on mathematical linguistics at mathematics seminars and colloquia. No one has ever asked me whether I have the appropriate credentials to speak on these subjects; the mathematicians couldn't care less. What they want to know is what I have to say. No one has ever objected to my right to speak, asking whether I have a doctor's degree in mathematics, or whether I have taken advanced courses in this subject. That would never have entered their minds. They want to know whether I am right or wrong, whether the subject is interesting or not, whether better approaches are possible—the discussion dealt with the subject, not with my right to discuss it.

But on the other hand, in discussion or debate concerning social issues or American foreign policy, Vietnam or the Middle East, for example, the issue is constantly raised, often with considerable venom. I've repeatedly been challenged on grounds of credentials, or asked, what special training do you have that entitles you to speak of these matters. The assumption is that people like me, who are outsiders from a professional viewpoint, are not entitled to speak on such things.

Compare mathematics and the political sciences—it's quite striking. In mathematics, in physics, people are concerned with what you say, not with your certification. But in order to speak about social reality, you must have the proper credentials, particularly if you depart from the accepted framework of thinking. Generally speaking, it seems fair to say that the richer the intellectual substance of a field, the less there is a concern for credentials, and the greater is the concern for content. One might even argue that to deal with substantive issues in the ideological disciplines may be a dangerous thing, because these disciplines are not simply concerned with discovering and explaining the facts as they are; rather, they tend to present these facts and interpret them in a manner that conforms to certain ideological requirements, and to become dangerous to established interests if they do not do so.

To complete the picture I should note a striking difference, in my personal experience at least, between the United States and other industrial democracies in this regard. Thus I have found over the years that although I am often asked to comment on international affairs or social issues by press, radio, and television in Canada, Western Europe, Japan, Australia, that is very rare in the United States.

(I exclude here the special pages of the newspapers in

which a range of dissenting view is permitted, even encouraged, but encapsulated and identified as "full expression of a range of opinion." I am referring rather to the commentary and analysis that enters into the mainstream of discussion and interpretation of contemporary affairs, a crucial difference.)

The contrast was quite dramatic through the period of the Vietnam War, and remains so today. If this were solely a personal experience, it would not be of any significance, but I am quite sure it is not. The United States is unusual among the industrial democracies in the rigidity of the system of ideological control—"indoctrination," we might say—exercised through the mass media. One of the devices used to achieve this narrowness of perspective is the reliance on professional credentials. The universities and academic disciplines have, in the past, been successful in safeguarding conformist attitudes and interpretations, so that by and large a reliance on "professional expertise" will ensure that views and analyses that depart from orthodoxy will rarely be expressed.

Thus, when I hesitate to try to link my work in linguistics to analyses of current affairs or of ideology, as many people suggest, it is for two reasons. In the first place, the connection is in fact tenuous. Furthermore, I do not want to contribute to the illusion that these questions require technical understanding, inaccessible without special training. But I don't want to deny what you say: one can approach the nature of ideology, the role of ideological control, the social role of the intelligentsia, etc., in a sophisticated fashion. But the task which confronts the ordinary citizen concerned with understanding social reality and removing the masks that disguise it is not comparable to Jean Pierre Faye's problem in his investigation of totalitarian language.

RONAT: In your analyses of ideology you have pointed to a "curious" fact: At times certain journals practice a policy of "balance," which consists of presenting contradictory reports or interpretations side by side. You said, however, that only the official version, that of the dominant ideology, was retained, even without proof, while the version of the opposition was rejected in spite of the evidence presented and the reliability of the sources.

CHOMSKY: Yes, in part because, obviously, privileged status is accorded to the version that conforms better to the needs of power and privilege. However, it is important not to overlook the tremendous imbalance as to how the social reality is presented to the public.

To my knowledge, in the American mass media you cannot find a single socialist journalist, not a single syndicated political commentator who is a socialist. From the ideological point of view the mass media are almost 100 percent "state capitalist." In a sense, we have over here the "mirror image" of the Soviet Union, where all the people who write in *Pravda* represent the position which they call "socialism"—in fact, a certain variety of highly authoritarian state socialism. Here in the United States there is an astonishing degree of ideological uniformity for such a complex country. Not a single socialist voice in the mass media, not even a timid one; perhaps there are some marginal exceptions, but I cannot think of any, offhand. Basically, there are two reasons for this. First, there is the remarkable ideological homogeneity of the American intelligentsia in general, who rarely depart from one of the variants of state capitalistic ideology (liberal or conservative), a fact which itself calls for explanation. The second reason is that the mass media are capitalist institutions. It is no doubt the same on the board of directors of General Motors. If no socialist is to be found on it—what would he be doing there!—it's not because they haven't been able to find anyone who is qualified. In a capitalist society the mass media are capitalist institutions. The fact that these institutions reflect the ideology of dominant economic interests is hardly surprising.

That is a crude and elementary fact. What you speak of points to more subtle phenomena. These, though interesting, must not make one forget the dominant factors.

It is notable that despite the extensive and well-known record of government lies during the period of the Vietnam War, the press, with fair consistency, remained remarkably obedient, and quite willing to accept the government's assumptions, framework of thinking, and interpretation of what was happening. Of course, on narrow technical questions—is the war succeeding? for example—the press was willing to criticize, and there were always honest correspondents in the field who described what they saw. But I am referring to the general pattern of interpretation and analysis, and to more general assumptions about what is right and proper. Furthermore, at times the press simply concealed easily documented facts—the bombing of Laos is a striking case.

But the subservience of the media is illustrated in less blatant ways as well. Take the peace treaty negotiations, revealed by Hanoi radio in October 1972, right before the November presidential elections. When Kissinger appeared on television to say that "peace is at hand," the press dutifully presented his version of what was happening, though even a cursory analysis of his comments showed that he was rejecting the basic principles of the negotiations on every crucial point, so that further escalation of the American war—as in fact took place with the Christmas bombings—was inevitable. I do not say this only with the benefit of hindsight. I and others exerted considerable energy trying to get the national press to face the obvious facts at the time, and I also wrote an article about it before the Christmas bombings,[1] which in particular predicted "increased terror bombing of North Vietnam."

The exact same story was replayed in January 1973, when the peace treaty was finally announced. Again Kissinger and the White House made it clear that the United States was rejecting every basic principle in the treaty it was signing, so that continued war was inevitable. The press dutifully accepted the official version, and even allowed some amazing falsehoods to stand unchallenged. I've discussed all of this in detail elsewhere.[2]

Or to mention another case, in an article written for *Ramparts*,[3] I reviewed the retrospective interpretations of the war in Vietnam presented in the press when the war came to an end in 1975—the liberal press, the rest is not interesting in this connection.

Virtually without exception, the press accepted the basic principles of government propaganda, without questioning them. Here we're talking about that part of the press which considered itself as opposed to the war. That's very striking. The same is often true of passionate critics of the war; presumably, to a large extent they aren't even conscious of it.

That applies particularly to those who are sometimes considered the "intellectual elite." There is, in fact, a curious book called *The American Intellectual Elite* by C. Kadushin, which

presents the results of an elaborate opinion survey of a group
identified as "the intellectual elite," undertaken in 1970. This
book contains a great deal of information on the group's attitudes toward the war at the time when opposition to the war
was at its peak. The overwhelming majority considered themselves to be opponents of the war, but in general for what they
called "pragmatic" reasons: they became convinced at a given
moment that the United States could not win at an acceptable
cost. I imagine a study of the "German intellectual elite"
in 1944 would have produced similar results. The study indi-
cates quite dramatically the remarkable degree of conformity and submission to the dominant ideology among people
who considered themselves informed critics of government
policy.

The consequence of this conformist subservience to those
in power, as Hans Morgenthau correctly termed it, is that in
the United States political discourse and debate have often
been less diversified even than in certain Fascist countries,
Franco Spain, for example, where there was lively discussion
covering a broad ideological range. Though the penalties for
deviance from official doctrine were incomparably more severe
than here, nevertheless opinion and thinking were not constrained within such narrow limits, a fact that frequently occa-
sioned surprise among Spanish intellectuals visiting the
United States during the latter years of the Franco period.
Much the same was true in Fascist Portugal, where there seem
to have been significant Marxist groups in the universities, to
mention just one example. The range and significance of the
ideological diversity became apparent with the fall of the dictatorship, and are also reflected in the liberation movements in

the Portuguese colonies—a two-way street, in that case, in that the Portuguese intellectuals were influenced by the liberation movements, and conversely, I suppose.

In the United States the situation is quite different. As compared with the other capitalist democracies, the United States is considerably more rigid and doctrinaire in its political thinking and analysis. Not only among the intelligentsia, though in this sector the fact is perhaps most striking. The United States is exceptional also in that there is no significant pressure for worker participation in management, let alone real workers' control. These issues are not alive in the United States, as they are throughout Western Europe. And the absence of any significant socialist voice or discussion is again quite a striking feature of the United States, as compared to other societies of comparable social structure and level of economic development.

Here one saw some small changes at the end of the sixties; but in 1965 you would have had great difficulty in finding a Marxist professor, or a socialist, in an economics department at a major university, for example. State capitalist ideology dominated the social sciences and every ideological discipline almost entirely. This conformism was called "the end of ideology." It dominated the professional fields—and still largely does—as well as the mass media and the journals of opinion. Such a degree of ideological conformity in a country which does not have a secret police, at least not much of one, and does not have concentration camps, is quite remarkable. Here the range of ideological diversity (the kind that implies lively debate on social issues) for many years has been very narrow, skewed much more to the right than in other industrial democracies. This is important. The subtleties to which you alluded must be considered within this framework.

Some changes did take place at the end of the sixties in the universities, largely due to the student movement, which demanded and achieved some broadening of the tolerated range of thinking. The reactions have been interesting. Now that the pressure of the student movement has been reduced, there is a substantial effort to reconstruct the orthodoxy that had been slightly disturbed. And constantly, in the discussions and the literature dealing with that period—often called "the time of troubles" or something of that sort—the student Left is depicted as a menace threatening freedom of research and teaching; the student movement is said to have placed the freedom of the universities in jeopardy by seeking to impose totalitarian ideological controls. That is how the state capitalist intellectuals describe the fact that their near total control of ideology was very briefly brought into question, as they seek to close again these slight breaches in the system of thought control, and to reverse the process through which just a little diversity arose within the ideological institutions: the totalitarian menace of fascism of the Left! And they really believe this, to such an extent have they been brainwashed and controlled by their own ideological commitments. One expects that from the police, but when it comes from the intellectuals, then that's very striking.

It is certainly true that there were some cases in the American universities when the actions of the students went beyond the limits of what is proper and legitimate. Some of the worst incidents, as we know now, were instigated by government provocateurs,[4] though a few, without doubt, represented excesses of the student movement itself. Those are the incidents on which many commentators focus their attention when they condemn the student movement.

The major effect of the student movement, however, was quite different, I believe. It raised a challenge to the subservience of the universities to the state and other external powers—although that challenge has not proven very effective, and this subordination has remained largely intact—and it managed to provoke, at times with some limited success, an opening in the ideological fields, thus bringing a slightly greater diversity of thought and study and research. In my opinion, it was this challenge to ideological control, mounted by the students (most of them liberals), chiefly in the social sciences, which induced such terror, verging at times on hysteria, in the reactions of the "intellectual elite." The analytic and retrospective studies which appear today often seem to me highly exaggerated and inexact in their account of the events that took place and their significance. Many intellectuals are seeking to reconstruct the orthodoxy and the control over thought and inquiry which they had institutionalized with such success, and which was in fact threatened—freedom is always a threat to the commissars.

RONAT: The student movement was first mobilized against the war in Vietnam, but did it not quite soon involve other issues?

CHOMSKY: The immediate issue was the Vietnam War, but also the civil rights movement of the preceding years—you must remember that the activists in the vanguard of the civil rights movement in the South had very often been students, for example, SNCC (Student Non-violent Coordinating Committee), which was a very important and effective group with a largely black leadership, and supported by many white students. Furthermore, some of the earlier issues had to do with opening up the campus to a greater range of thought and to political activity of diverse tendencies, as in the Berkeley free speech controversy.

It did not seem to me at the time that the student activists were really trying to "politicize" the universities. During the period when the domination of faculty ideologues was not yet at issue, the universities were highly politicized and made regular and significant contributions to external powers, especially to the government, its programs, and its policies; this continued to be true during the period of the student movement, just as it is today. It would be more exact to say that the student movement, from the beginning, tried to open up the universities and free them from outside control. To be sure, from the point of view of those who had subverted the universities and converted them to a significant extent into instruments of government policy and official ideology this effort appeared to be an illegitimate form of "politicization." All of this seems obvious as regards university laboratories devoted to weapons production or social science programs with intimate connections to counterinsurgency, government intelligence services and propaganda, and social control. It is less obvious, perhaps, but nevertheless true, I think, in the domain of academic scholarship.

To illustrate this, take the example of the history of the cold war, and the so-called revisionist interpretation of the period following World War II. The "revisionists," as you know, were those American commentators who opposed the official "orthodox" version. This orthodoxy, quite dominant at the time, held that the cold war was due solely to Russian and Chinese aggressiveness, and that the United States played a passive role, merely reacting to this. This position was adopted by even the most liberal commentators. Take a man like John Kenneth Galbraith, who within the liberal establishment has long been one of the most open, questioning, and skeptical minds, one of those who tried to break out of the orthodox framework on many issues. Well, in his book *The New Industrial State*, published in 1967—as late as that!—where he lays much stress on the open and critical attitude of the intelligentsia and the encouraging prospects this offers, he says that "the undoubted historical source" of the cold war was Russian and Chinese aggressiveness: "the revolutionary and national aspirations of the Soviets, and more recently of the Chinese, and the compulsive vigor of their assertion."[5] That is what the liberal critics were still saying in 1967.

The "revisionist" alternative was developed in various conflicting versions by James Warburg, D.F. Fleming, William Appleman Williams, Gar Alperovitz, Gabriel Kolko, David Horowitz, Diane Clemens, and others. They argued that the cold war resulted from an interaction of great power designs and suspicions. This position not only has prima facie plausibility, but also receives strong support from the historical and documentary record. But few people paid much attention to "revisionist" studies, which were often the object of scorn or a few pleasantries among "serious" analysts.

By the end of the sixties, however, it had become impossible to prevent serious consideration of the "revisionist" position, in large part because of the pressures of the student movement. Students had read these books and wanted to have them discussed. What resulted is quite interesting.

In the first place, as soon as the revisionist alternative was seriously considered, the orthodox position simply dissolved, vanished. As soon as the debate was opened, it found itself lacking an object, virtually. The orthodox position was abandoned.

To be sure, orthodox historians rarely admitted that they had been in error. Instead, while adopting some of the revisionist views, they attributed to the revisionists a stupid position, according to which—to take a not untypical characterization—"the Soviet Government ... was merely the hapless object of our vicious diplomacy." This is Herbert Feis's rendition of the position of Gar Alperovitz, whose actual view was that "the Cold War cannot be understood simply as an American response to a Soviet challenge, but rather as the insidious interaction of mutual suspicions, blame for which must be shared by all." Quite typically, the view attributed to the revisionists was a nonsensical one that takes no account of interaction of the superpowers. Orthodox historians took over some elements of the revisionist analysis, while attributing to them an idiotic doctrine that was fundamentally different from what had actually been proposed, and in fact was the mirror image of the original orthodox position. The motivation for this mode of argument is of course obvious enough.

Starting from this slightly revised basis, many orthodox historians have sought to reconstruct the image of American benevolence and passivity. But I do not want to go into this development here. As for the impact of the revisionist analysis, Galbraith again provides an interesting example: I have already quoted his book, which appeared in 1967. In a revised edition, in 1971, he replaced the word "the" by the word "an" in the passage quoted: "the revolutionary and national aspirations of the Soviets, and more recently of the Chinese, and the compulsive vigor of their assertion, were *an* undoubted historical source [of the cold war]" (my emphasis). This account is still misleading and biased, because he does not speak of the *other* causes; it would also be interesting to see in just what way the initiatives of China were "an undoubted source" of the cold war. But the position is at least tenable, in contrast to the orthodox position, which he gave in the previous edition four years earlier—and prior to the general impact of the student movement on the universities.

Galbraith is an interesting example just because he is one of the most open, critical, and questioning minds among the liberal intelligentsia. His comments on the cold war and its origins are also interesting because they are presented as a casual side remark: he does not attempt in this context to give an original historical analysis, but merely reports in passing the doctrine accepted among those liberal intellectuals who were somewhat skeptical and critical. We are not talking here about an Arthur Schlesinger or other ideologues who at times present a selection of historical facts in a manner comparable to the party historians of other faiths.

One can understand why so many liberal intellectuals were terrified at the end of the sixties, why they describe this period as one of totalitarianism of the Left: for once they were compelled to look the world of facts in the face. A serious threat, and a real danger for people whose role is ideological control. There is a recent and quite interesting study put out by the

Trilateral Commission—*The Crisis of Democracy*, by Michel Crozier, Samuel Huntington, and Joji Watanuki—in which an international group of scholars and others discuss what they see as contemporary threats to democracy. One of these threats is posed by "value-oriented intellectuals" who, as they correctly point out, often challenge the institutions that are responsible for "the indoctrination of the young"—an apt phrase. The student movement contributed materially to this aspect of "the crisis of democracy."

By the late sixties the discussion had gone beyond the question of Vietnam or the interpretation of contemporary history; it concerned the *institutions* themselves. Orthodox economics was very briefly challenged by students who wanted to undertake a fundamental critique of the functioning of the capitalist economy; students questioned the institutions, they wanted to study Marx and political economy.

Perhaps I can illustrate this once again with a personal anecdote:

In the spring of 1969 a small group of students in economics here in Cambridge wanted to initiate a discussion of the nature of economics as a field of study. In order to open this discussion, they tried to organize a debate in which the two main speakers would be Paul Samuelson, the eminent Keynesian economist at MIT (today a Nobel laureate), and a Marxist economist. But for this latter role they were not able to find anyone in the Boston area, no one who was willing to question the neoclassical position from the point of view of Marxist political economy. Finally I was asked to take on the task, though I have no particular knowledge of economics, and no commitment to Marxism. Not one professional, or even semi-professional, in 1969! And Cambridge is a very lively place in these respects. That may give you some idea of the prevailing intellectual climate. It is difficult to imagine anything comparable in Western Europe or Japan.

The student movement changed these things to a small extent: what was described, as I told you, as terror at the university . . . the SS marching through the corridors . . . the academic intelligentsia barely survived these terrifying attacks by student radicals . . . of course, due solely to their great courage. Unbelievable fantasies! Although, to be sure, there were incidents, sometimes instigated by provocateurs of the FBI, as we know now, which stimulated that paranoid interpretation. What a devastating thing, to have opened up the university just a little! But the mass media were hardly touched at all, and now orthodoxy has been reestablished, because the pressure is no longer there. For example, a serious diplomatic historian like Gaddis Smith can now describe Williams and Kolko as "pamphleteers" in the *New York Times Book Review.*

RONAT: To what do you attribute this "falling off" of the pressure?

CHOMSKY: To many things. When the New Left developed within the student movement in the United States, it could not associate itself with any broader social movement, rooted in any important segment of the population. In large part this was the result of the ideological narrowness of the preceding period. Students form a social group that is marginal and transitory. The student Left constituted a small minority, often confronted by very difficult circumstances. A living intellectual tradition of the Left did not exist, nor a socialist movement with a base in the working class. There was no living tradition or popular movement from which they could gain support. Under these circumstances, it is perhaps surprising that the student movement lasted as long as it did.

RONAT: And the new generation?

CHOMSKY: It is faced with new forms of experience. Students today seem to find it easier to adapt to the demands imposed from the outside, though one should not exaggerate; in my experience at least, colleges are quite unlike the fifties and early sixties. The economic stagnation and recession have a lot to do with student attitudes. Under the conditions of the sixties students could suppose that they would find means of subsistence, no matter what they did. The society seemed to have sufficient interstices, there was a sense of expansiveness and optimism, so that one could hope to find a place somehow. Now that is no longer the case. Even those who are "disciplined" and well prepared professionally may become well-educated taxi drivers. Student activism has felt the effect of all this.

Other factors have also played a role. There is evidence that certain universities, perhaps many of them, have explicitly sought to exclude leftist students. Even in liberal universities, political criteria have been imposed to exclude students who might "cause problems." Not entirely, of course, otherwise they would have excluded all the good students. Leftist students also have had serious difficulties in working at the universities, or later, in gaining appointments, at least in the ideological disciplines, political science, economics, Asian studies, for example.

RONAT: At the time of the French publication of your book *Counterrevolutionary Violence (Bains de Sang)* there was much talk in France about the fact that the English original had been censored (that is, distribution was blocked) by the conglomerate to which the publishing house belonged; the publishing house itself was closed and its personnel dismissed. The chief editor became a taxi driver and now is organizing a taxi-drivers' union. French television has cast doubt on this story.

CHOMSKY: That "censorship" by the conglomerate did take place, as you describe, but it was a stupid act on their part. At that level censorship isn't necessary, given the number of potential readers on the one hand, and on the other, the weight exerted by the enormous ideological apparatus. I have often thought that if a rational Fascist dictatorship were to exist, then it would choose the American system. State censorship is not necessary, or even very efficient, in comparison to the ideological controls exercised by systems that are more complex and more decentralized.

RONAT: Within this framework, how do you interpret the Watergate affair, which has often been presented in France as the "triumph" of democracy?

CHOMSKY: To consider the Watergate affair as a triumph of democracy is an error, in my opinion. The real question raised was not, Did Nixon employ evil methods against his political adversaries? but rather, Who were the victims? The answer is clear. Nixon was condemned, not because he employed reprehensible methods in his political struggles, but because he made a mistake in the choice of adversaries against whom he turned these methods. *He attacked people with power.*

The telephone taps? Such practices have existed for a long time. He had an "enemies list"? But nothing happened to those who were on that list. I was on that list, nothing happened to me. No, he simply made a mistake in his choice of enemies: he had on his list the chairman of IBM, senior government advisers, distinguished pundits of the press, highly placed supporters of the Democratic Party. He attacked the *Washington Post,* a major capitalist enterprise. And these powerful people defended themselves at once, as would be expected. Watergate? Men of power against men of power.

Similar crimes, and others much graver, could have been charged against other people as well as Nixon. But those crimes were typically directed against minorities or against movements of social change, and few ever protested. The ideological censorship kept these matters from the public eye during the Watergate period, although remarkable documentation concerning this repression appeared at just this time. It was only when the dust of Watergate had settled that the press and the political commentators turned toward some of the real and profound cases of abuse of state power—still without recognizing or exploring the gravity of the issue.

For example, the Church Committee has published information, the significance of which has not really been made clear. At the time of its revelations, a great deal of publicity was focused on the Martin Luther King affair, but still more important revelations have hardly been dealt with by the press to this day (January 1976). For example, the following: In Chicago there was a street gang called the Blackstone Rangers, which

operated in the ghetto. The Black Panthers were in contact
with them, attempting to politicize them, it appears. As long as
the Rangers remained a ghetto street gang—a criminal gang,
as depicted by the FBI, at least—the FBI were not much
concerned; this was also a way of controlling the ghetto. But
radicalized into a political group, they became potentially
dangerous.

The basic function of the FBI is not to stop crime. Rather,
it functions as a political police, in large measure. An indication
is given by the FBI budget and the way it is apportioned. Some
suggestive information on this subject has been revealed by a
group calling themselves the "Citizens' Commission to Investigate the FBI," who succeeded in stealing from the FBI's Media,
Pennsylvania, office a collection of documents which they attempted to circulate to the press. The breakdown of these documents was approximately the following: 30 percent were
devoted to routine procedures; 40 percent to political surveillance involving two right-wing groups, ten groups concerned
with immigrants, and more than two hundred liberal or left-
wing groups; 14 percent to AWOLs and deserters; 1 percent to
organized crime—mostly gambling—and the rest to rape,
bank robbery, murder, etc.

Faced with the potential alliance of the Rangers and the
Black Panthers, the FBI decided to take action, in line with the
national program of dismantling the Left in which it was engaged, the national counterintelligence program known as
COINTELPRO. They sought to incite conflict between the
two groups by means of a forgery, an anonymous letter sent
to the leader of the Rangers by someone who identified himself
as "a black brother." This letter warned of a Panther plot to

assassinate the leader of the Rangers. Its transparent purpose was to incite the Rangers—described in FBI documents as a group "to whom violent type activity, shooting, and the like, are second nature"—to respond with violence to the fictitious assassination plot.

But it didn't work, perhaps because at that time the relations between the Rangers and the Panthers were already too close. The FBI had to take on the task of destroying the Panthers itself. How?

Though there has been no systematic investigation, we can reconstruct what seems to be a plausible story:

A few months later, in December 1969, the Chicago police conducted a pre-dawn raid on a Panther apartment. Approximately one hundred shots were fired. At first the police claimed that they had responded to the fire of the Panthers, but it was quickly established by the local press that this was false. Fred Hampton, one of the most talented and promising leaders of the Panthers, was killed in his bed. There is evidence that he may have been drugged. Witnesses claim that he was murdered in cold blood. Mark Clark was also killed. This event can fairly be described as a Gestapo-style political assassination.

At the time it was thought that the Chicago police were behind the raid. That would have been bad enough, but the facts revealed since suggest something more sinister. We know today that Hampton's personal bodyguard, William O'Neal, who was also chief of Panther security, was an FBI infiltrator. A few days before the raid, the FBI office turned over to the Chicago police a floor plan of the Panther apartment supplied by O'Neal, with the location of the beds marked, along with a rather dubious report by O'Neal that illegal weapons were kept in the apartment: the pretext for the raid. Perhaps the floor plan explains the fact, noticed by reporters, that the police gunfire was directed to inside corners of the apartment rather than the entrances. It certainly undermines still further the original pretense that the police were firing in response to Panther gunshots, confused by unfamiliar surroundings. The Chicago press has reported that the FBI agent to whom O'Neal reported was the head of Chicago COINTELPRO directed against the Black Panthers and other black groups. Whether or not this is true, there is direct evidence of FBI complicity in the murders.

Putting this information together with the documented effort of the FBI to incite violence and gang warfare a few months earlier, it seems not unreasonable to speculate that the FBI undertook on its own initiative the murder that it could not elicit from the "violence-prone" group to which it had addressed a fabricated letter implicating the Panthers in an assassination attempt against its leader.

This one incident (which, incidentally, was not seriously investigated by the Church Committee) completely overshadows the entire Watergate episode in significance by a substantial margin. But with a few exceptions the national press or television have had little to say on the subject, though it has been well covered locally in Chicago. The matter has rarely been dealt with by political commentators. The comparison with coverage of such "atrocities" as Nixon's "enemies list" or tax trickery is quite striking. For example, during the entire Watergate period, the *New Republic*, which was then virtually the official organ of American liberalism, found no occasion to report or comment on these matters, although the basic facts and documents had become known.

The family of Fred Hampton brought a civil suit against the Chicago police, but up to the present the FBI involvement has been excluded from the courts, although much relevant information is available in depositions made under oath.

If people offended by "Watergate horrors" were really concerned with civil and human rights, they should have pursued the information released by the Church Committee with regard to the affair of the Blackstone Rangers, and considered the possible relevance of this information to what is known concerning FBI involvement in the murder of Fred Hampton by the Chicago police. At least a serious inquiry should have been initiated to examine what seem to be possible connections, and to bring to light the FBI role under Nixon and his predecessors. For what was at issue here was an assassination in which the national political police may have been implicated, a crime that far transcends anything attributed to Nixon in the Watergate investigations. I should recall that the Watergate inquiry did touch on one issue of extraordinary importance, the bombing of Cambodia, but only on very narrow grounds—it was the alleged "secrecy" of the bombings, not the fact itself, that was charged to Nixon as his "crime" in this regard.

There are other cases of this kind. For example, in San Diego the FBI apparently financed, armed, and controlled an extreme right-wing group of former Minute Men, transforming it into something called the Secret Army Organization specializing in terrorist acts of various kinds. I heard of this first from one of my former students, who was the target of an assassination attempt by the organization. In fact, he is the student who had organized the debate on economics that I told you about a little while ago, when he was still a student at MIT.

Now he was teaching at San Diego State College and was engaged in political activities—which incidentally were completely nonviolent, not that this is relevant.

The head of the Secret Army Organization—a provocateur in the pay of the FBI—drove past his house, and his companion fired shots into it, seriously wounding a young woman. The young man who was their target was not at home at the time. The weapon had been stolen by this FBI provocateur. According to the local branch of the ACLU, the gun was handed over the next day to the San Diego FBI Bureau, which hid it; and for six months the FBI lied to the San Diego police about the incident. This affair did not become publicly known until later.

This terrorist group, directed and financed by the FBI, was finally broken up by the San Diego police, after they had tried to fire-bomb a theater in the presence of police. The FBI agent in question, who had hidden the weapon, was transferred outside the state of California so that he could not be prosecuted. The FBI provocateur also escaped prosecution, though several members of the secret terrorist organization were prosecuted. The FBI was engaged in efforts to incite gang warfare among black groups in San Diego, as in Chicago, at about the same time. In secret documents, the FBI took credit for inciting shootings, beatings, and unrest in the ghetto, a fact that has elicited very little comment in the press or journals of opinion.

This same young man, incidentally, was harassed in other ways. It appears that the FBI continued to subject him to various kinds of intimidation and threats, by means of provocateurs. Furthermore, according to his ACLU attorneys, the FBI supplied information to the college where he was teaching that was the basis for misconduct charges filed against him. He faced three successive inquiries at the college, and each time was absolved of the charges brought against him. At that point the chancellor of the California state college system, Glenn Dumke, stated that he would not accept the findings of the independent hearing committees and simply dismissed him from his position. Notice that such incidents, of which there have been a fair number, are not regarded as "totalitarianism" in the university.

The basic facts were submitted to the Church Committee by the ACLU in June 1975 and also offered to the press. As far as I know, the committee did not conduct any investigation into the matter. The national press said virtually nothing about these incidents at the time, and very little since.

There have been similar reports concerning other government programs of repression. For example, Army Intelligence has been reported to have engaged in illegal actions in Chicago. In Seattle, fairly extensive efforts were undertaken to disrupt and discredit local left-wing groups. The FBI ordered one of its agents to induce a group of young radicals to blow up a bridge; this was to be done in such a manner that the person who was to plant the bomb would also be blown up with it. The agent refused to carry out these instructions. Instead, he talked to the press and finally testified in court. That is how the matter became known. In Seattle, FBI infiltrators were inciting arson, terrorism, and bombing, and in one case entrapped a young black man in a robbery attempt, which they initiated and in the course of which he was killed. This was reported by Frank Donner in the *Nation*, one of the few American journals to have attempted some serious coverage of such matters.

There is a good deal more of this. But all these isolated

cases only take on their full meaning if you put them into the context of the policies of the FBI since its origins during the post–World War I Red scare, which I will not try to review here. The COINTELPRO operations began in the 1950s, with a program to disrupt and destroy the Communist Party. Although this was not officially proclaimed, everybody knew something of the sort was going on, and there were very few protests; it was considered quite legitimate. People even joked about it.

In 1960 the disruption program was extended to the Puerto Rican independence movement. In October 1961, under the administration of Attorney General Robert Kennedy, the FBI initiated a disruption program against the Socialist Workers Party (the largest Trotskyist organization); the program was later extended to the civil rights movement, the Ku Klux Klan, black nationalist groups, and the peace movement in general; by 1968 it covered the entire "New Left."

The rationale given internally for these illegal programs is quite revealing. The program for disrupting the Socialist Workers Party, which came directly from the central office of the FBI, presented its rationale in essentially these terms:

We launch this program for the following reasons:
(1) the Socialist Workers Party is openly running candidates in local elections throughout the country;
(2) it supports integration in the South;
(3) it supports Castro.

What does this actually indicate? It means that SWP political initiative in running candidates in elections—*legal* political activity—their work in support of civil rights, and their efforts to change U.S. foreign policy justify their destruction at the hands of the national political police.

This is the rationale behind these programs of government repression: they were directed against civil rights activities and against legal political action that ran counter to the prevailing consensus. In comparison with COINTELPRO and related government actions in the 1960s, Watergate was a tea party. It is instructive, however, to compare the relative attention accorded to them in the press. This comparison reveals clearly and dramatically that it was the improper choice of targets, not improper acts, that led to Nixon's downfall. The alleged concern for civil and democratic rights was a sham. There was no "triumph of democracy."

RONAT: It appears that a proposal, containing passages from the Constitution of the United States and the Bill of Rights, was distributed in the streets at one time and people refused to sign it, believing it to be left-wing propaganda.

CHOMSKY: Such incidents have been reported from the 1950s, if I recall. People have been intimidated for many years. Liberals would like to believe that all of this is due to a few evil men: Joe McCarthy and Richard Nixon. That is quite false. One can trace the postwar repression to security measures initiated by Truman in 1947, and efforts by Democratic liberals to discredit Henry Wallace and his supporters at that time. It was the liberal senator Hubert Humphrey who proposed detention camps in case of a "national emergency." He did finally vote against the McCarran Act but said at the time that he found it not sufficiently harsh in some respects; he was opposed to the provision that prisoners in the detention camps should be protected by the right of habeas corpus: that was not the way to treat Communist conspirators! The Communist Control Act introduced by leading liberals a few years later was so patently unconstitutional that no one actually tried to enforce it, to my knowledge. This law, incidentally, was specifically directed in part against trade unions. And together with these senators, many liberal intellectuals implicitly supported the fundamental aims of "McCarthyism," though they objected to his methods—particularly when they, too, became targets. They carried out what amounted to a partial "purge" in the universities, and in many ways developed the ideological framework for ridding American society of this "cancer" of serious dissent. These are among the reasons for the remarkable conformism and ideological narrowness of intellectual life in the United States, and for the isolation of the student movement that we discussed earlier.

If these liberals opposed McCarthy, it was because he went too far, and in the wrong way. He attacked the liberal intelligentsia themselves, or mainstream political figures like George Marshall, instead of confining himself to the "Communist enemy." Like Nixon, he made a mistake in choosing his enemies when he began to attack the church and the army. Commonly, if liberal intellectuals criticized him, it was on the grounds that his methods were not the right ones for ridding the country of real communists. There were some notable exceptions, but depressingly few.

Similarly, Justice Robert Jackson, one of the leading liberals on the Supreme Court, opposed the doctrine of "clear and present danger" (according to which freedom of speech could be abridged in cases affecting the security of the state) when applied to Communist activities, because it was not harsh enough. If you wait until the danger becomes "clear and present," he explained, it will be too late. You must stop Communists *before* their "imminent actions." Thus he supported a truly totalitarian point of view: We must not permit this kind of discussion to begin.

But these liberals were very shocked when McCarthy turned his weapons against them. He was no longer playing according to the rules of the game—the game that they invented.

RONAT: Similarly, I've noticed that the scandal involving the CIA did not concern the main activities of the agency, but the fact that it did work which in principle was the assigned sphere of the FBI.

CHOMSKY: In part, yes. And look at the furor that has arisen over the attempts at political assassination organized by the CIA. People were shocked because the CIA tried to assassinate foreign leaders. Certainly, that is very bad. But these were only abortive attempts; at least in most cases—in some it is not so clear. Consider in comparison the Phoenix program in which the CIA was involved, which, according to the Saigon government, exterminated forty thousand civilians within two years. Why doesn't that count? Why are all these people less significant than Castro or Schneider or Lumumba?

The official who was responsible for this, William Colby, who headed the CIA, is now a respected columnist and lecturer on university campuses. The same thing happened in Laos, though even worse. How many peasants were killed as a result of CIA programs? And who speaks of this? Nobody. No headlines.

It's always the same story. The crimes that are exposed are significant, but they are trivial as compared to the really serious criminal programs of the state, which are ignored or regarded as quite legitimate.

RONAT: How do you find all this information? If the newspapers don't report it . . .

CHOMSKY: This information is accessible, but only for *fanatics:* in order to unearth it, you have to devote much of your life to the search. In that sense the information is accessible. But this "accessibility" is hardly significant in practice. It is politically more or less irrelevant. All the same, on the personal level, the situation for someone like me is of course incomparably preferable in the United States to the totalitarian societies. In the Soviet Union, for example, someone who tried to do what I do here would probably be in prison. It is interesting, and typical, that my political writings critical of U.S. policies are never translated in the so-called Communist countries, though they are, quite widely, in many other parts of the world. But one must be cautious in assessing the political significance of the relative freedom from repression—at least for the privileged—in the United States. Exactly what does it mean, concretely?

For example, last year I was invited to give a lecture at Harvard before a group of journalists called the Nieman Fellows, who come there each year from all over the United States and foreign countries in order to further their education, so to speak. They asked me to discuss Watergate and related topics—the press generally was quite proud of its courageous and principled behavior during the Watergate period, for very little reason, as I've just tried to explain. Instead of discussing Watergate, I spoke about the things to which I've just alluded, because I wondered to what extent these journalists, who are quite sophisticated and well informed compared to the general population, might know about these matters. Well, none of them had any idea of the scale of the FBI programs of repression, except for one journalist from Chicago, who knew all about the Hampton affair. That had indeed been discussed in detail in the Chicago press. If there had been someone from San Diego in the group, he would have known about the Secret Army Organization, and so forth . . .

That is one of the keys to the whole thing. Everyone is led to think that what he knows represents a local exception. *But the overall pattern remains hidden.* Information is often given in the local papers, but its general significance, the patterns on the national level, remain obscured. That was the case during the entire Watergate period, although the information appeared just at that time, in its essentials, and with extensive documentation. And even since then the discussion has rarely been analytic or anywhere near comprehensive, and has not accounted for what happened in a satisfactory manner. What you face here is a very effective kind of ideological control, because one can remain under the impression that censorship does not exist, and in a narrow technical sense that is correct. You will not be imprisoned if you discover the facts, not even if you proclaim them whenever you can. But the results remain much the same as if there were real censorship. Social reality is generally concealed by the intelligentsia. Of course matters were quite different during the period when there was an enormous popular anti-war and student movement. Within the structure of popular movements there were many possibilities for expressing views that departed from the narrow limits of more or less "official" ideology, to which the intelligentsia generally conform.

RONAT: What was the reaction of Americans to the statements of Solzhenitsyn?

CHOMSKY: Very interesting—at least in the liberal press, which is what primarily concerns me. Some criticized his extravagances. He went well beyond what they could tolerate. For example, he called for direct intervention by the United States in the USSR—of a sort that could very well lead to war and, far short of that, is likely to harm the Russian dissidents themselves. Also, he denounced American weakness in abandoning the struggle to subdue the Vietnamese resistance, publicly opposed democratic reforms in Spain, supported a journal that called for censorship in the United States, and so on. Nonetheless, the press never ceased marveling at what an absolute moral giant this man was. In our petty lives, we can barely imagine such heights of moral grandeur.

In fact, the "moral level" of Solzhenitsyn is quite comparable to that of many American Communists who have fought courageously for civil liberties here in their own country, while at the same time defending, or refusing to criticize, the purges and labor camps in the Soviet Union. Sakharov is not as outlandish in his views as Solzhenitsyn, certainly, but he too says that it was a great setback for the West not to have pursued the Vietnam War to an American victory. The United States did not act with sufficient resolution and delayed too long in sending a large expeditionary force, he complains. Every fabrication of the U.S. propaganda apparatus is repeated, just as American Communists who have struggled for civil rights here parrot Russian propaganda. The easily documented fact of American aggression in South Vietnam is not part of history, for example. One must admire Sakharov's great courage and his fine work in defense of human rights in the Soviet Union. But to refer to such people as "moral giants" is quite remarkable.

Why do they do this? Because it is extremely important for mainstream American intellectuals to make people believe that the United States does not confront any real moral problems. Such problems only arise in the Soviet Union, and the "moral giants" are there to respond to them.

Compare Solzhenitsyn to many thousands of Vietnam War resisters and deserters; many of them acted at a moral level that is incomparably superior to his. Solzhenitsyn resolutely defends his own rights and those of people like him—which is certainly admirable. The resisters and many deserters defended the *rights of others*—namely, the victims of American aggression and terror. Their actions were on a much higher moral plane. Furthermore, their actions were not merely a response to their own persecution; for the most part they undertook these actions, which led to imprisonment or exile, of their own free will, when they could have easily lived in comfort. Yet we read in the American liberal journals that we can hardly conceive of the moral grandeur of Solzhenitsyn in our society, and surely can find no one like him. A very interesting pretense, with many implications.

It is quite generally claimed now that the American resistance had as its cause the young men's fear of being drafted; that's a very convenient belief for the intellectuals who confined themselves to "pragmatic" opposition to the war. But it is an enormous lie. For most of those who were in the resistance from its origins, nothing would have been easier than to escape the draft, with its class bias, as many others actually did. In fact, many of the activists already had deferments. Many of the deserters, too, chose a difficult and painful course for reasons of principle. But for those who supported the war initially, and who only raised their whisper of protest when the costs became too great, it is impossible to admit the existence of a courageous and principled resistance, largely on the part of youth, to the atrocities which they themselves had readily tolerated. The mainstream of American liberalism does not wish to hear anything about all that. It would raise too many embarrassing questions: What were they doing when the war resisters were facing prison or exile? And so on. So Solzhenitsyn comes to them as a gift of God, which permits them to evade moral questions, "exporting them," so to speak, and to conceal their own role as people who remained silent for so many years, or finally objected on narrow and morally repugnant grounds of cost and U.S. government interest.

Moynihan, when he was ambassador to the United Nations, produced the same effect when he attacked the Third World. These attacks aroused great admiration here; for example, when he denounced Idi Amin of Uganda as a "racist murderer." The question is not whether Idi Amin is a racist murderer. No doubt the appelation is correct. The question is, what does it mean for Moynihan to make this accusation and for others to applaud his honesty and courage in doing so?

Who is Moynihan? He served in four administrations, those of Kennedy, Johnson, Nixon, and Ford—that is to say, administrations that were guilty of racist murder on a scale undreamed of by Idi Amin. Imagine that some minor functionary of the Third Reich had correctly accused someone of being a racist murderer. This manner of shifting moral issues to others is one of the ways to reconstruct the foundations of moral legitimacy for the exercise of American power, shaken during the Vietnam War. Solzhenitsyn is exploited to this end in a natural and predictable way, though of course one cannot on those grounds draw any conclusions in regard to his charges against the Soviet system of oppression and violence.

Think of someone like Angela Davis: she defends the rights of American blacks with great courage and conviction. At the same time she refused to defend Czech dissidents or to criticize the Russian invasion of Czechoslovakia. Is she regarded as a "moral giant"? Hardly. Yet I believe she is superior to Solzhenitsyn on the moral level. At least she did not reproach the Soviet Union for not having conducted its atrocities with sufficient vigor.

RONAT: After what you have said, and what is said about the U.S. intervention in Chile in Uribe's book,[6] there apparently exists a veritable policy of *vaccination*. Deliberately a major scandal is exploded about a minor event—Watergate, the ITT case in 1973—in order to better hide and render more *acceptable* (according to Faye's definition) the true scandals: political assassinations, the coup d'état of September. You inoculate the public with a minor scandal; then when more serious things happen, the subject has already been deprived of most of its sensation value, its topical importance no longer has the aspect of novelty—the two fundamental criteria for big headlines in the newspapers.[7]

CHOMSKY: Yes, that is in keeping with what I've just said about the liberal press since the end of the war. The government has great need now to restore its credibility, to make people forget history, and to rewrite it. The intelligentsia have to a remarkable degree undertaken this task. It is also necessary to establish the "lessons" that have to be drawn from the war, to ensure that these are conceived on the narrowest grounds, in terms of such socially neutral categories as "stupidity" or "error" or "ignorance" or perhaps "cost."

Why? Because soon it will be necessary to justify other confrontations, perhaps other U.S. interventions in the world, other Vietnams.

But this time, these will have to be successful interventions, which don't slip out of control. Chile, for example. It is even possible for the press to criticize successful interventions—the Dominican Republic, Chile, etc.—as long as these criticisms don't exceed "civilized limits," that is to say, as long as they don't serve to arouse popular movements capable of hindering these enterprises, and are not accompanied by any rational analysis of the motives of U.S. imperialism, something which is complete anathema, intolerable to liberal ideology.

How is the liberal press proceeding with regard to Vietnam, that sector which supported the "doves"? By stressing the "stupidity" of the U.S. intervention; that's a politically neutral term. It would have been sufficient to find an "intelligent" policy. The war was thus a tragic error in which good intentions were transmuted into bad policies, because of a generation of incompetent and arrogant officials. The war's savagery is also denounced; but that, too, is used as a neutral category . . . Presumably the goals were legitimate—it would have been all right to do the same thing, but more humanely . . .

The "responsible" doves were opposed to the war—on a pragmatic basis. Now it is necessary to reconstruct the system of beliefs according to which the United States is the benefactor of humanity, historically committed to freedom, self-determination, and human rights. With regard to this doctrine, the "responsible" doves share the same presuppositions as the hawks: they do not question the right of the United States to intervene in other countries. Their criticism is actually very convenient for the state, which is quite willing to be chided for its errors, as long as the fundamental right of forceful intervention is not brought into question.

Take a look at this editorial in the *New York Times*, offering a retrospective analysis of the Vietnam War as it came to an end. The editors feel that it is too early to draw conclusions about the war:

> Clio, the goddess of history, is cool and slow and elusive in her ways. . . . Only later, much later, can history begin to make an assessment of the mixture of good and evil, of wisdom and folly, of ideals and illusions in the long Vietnam story. . . . There are those Americans who believe that the war to preserve a non-Communist, independent South Vietnam could have been waged differently. There are other Americans who believe that a viable, non-Communist South Vietnam was always a myth. . . . A decade of fierce polemics has failed to resolve this ongoing quarrel.

You see, they don't even mention the logical possibility of a third position: namely, that the United States did not have the right, either the legal or the moral right, to intervene by force in the internal affairs of Vietnam. We leave to history the task of judging the debate between the hawks and the respectable doves, but the third position, opposed to the other two, is excluded from discussion. The sphere of Clio does not extend to such absurd ideas as the belief that the United States has no unique right to intervene with force in the internal affairs of others, whether such intervention is successful or not. The *Times* published many letters responding to its editorial, but no letter questioning the alternatives presented. I know for certain that at least one such letter was sent to them . . . quite possibly many others.

April 8, 1975

To the Editor
New York Times
229 West 43d St.
New York, N.Y. 10036

Dear Sir:

An editorial in the *Times*, April 5, observes that "a decade of fierce polemics has failed to resolve this ongoing quarrel" between two contending views: that "the war to preserve a non-Communist, independent South Vietnam could have been waged differently," and that "a viable, non-Communist South Vietnam was always a myth." There has also been a third position: That apart from its prospects for success, the United States has neither the authority nor competence to intervene in the internal affairs of Vietnam. This was the position of much of the authentic peace movement, that is, those who opposed the war because it was wrong, not merely because it was unsuccessful. It is regrettable that this position is not even a contender in the debate, as the *Times* sees it.

On a facing page, Donald Kirk observes that "since the term 'bloodbath' first came into vogue in the Indochinese conflict, no one seems to have applied it to the war itself— only to the possible consequences of ending the war." He is quite wrong. Many Americans involved in the authentic peace movement have insisted for years on the elementary point that he believes has been noticed by "no one," and it is a commonplace in literature on the war. To mention just one example, we have written a small book on the subject (*Counterrevolutionary Violence: Bloodbaths in Fact and Propaganda*, 1973), though in this case the corporation (Warner Brothers) that owned the publisher refused to permit distribution after publication. But quite apart from this, the observation has been made repeatedly in discussion and literature on the war, by just that segment of opinion that the *Times* editorial excludes from the debate.

Sincerely yours,

Noam Chomsky
Professor, MIT

Edward S. Herman
Professor, University
of Pennsylvania

NC/ESH: lt

Note that as the *Times* sets the spectrum of debate, the position of much of the peace movement is simply excluded from consideration. Not that it is wrong, but rather unthinkable, inexpressible. As the *Times* sets the ground rules, the basic premises of the state propaganda system are presupposed by all participants in the debate: the American goal was to preserve an "independent" South Vietnam—perfect nonsense, as is easy to demonstrate—and the only question that arises is whether this worthy goal was within our grasp or not. Even the more audacious propaganda systems rarely go so far as to put forth state doctrine as unquestionable dogma, so that criticism of it need not even be rejected, but may simply be ignored.

Here we have a marvelous illustration of the functioning of propaganda in a democracy. A totalitarian state simply enunciates official doctrine—clearly, explicitly. Internally, one can think what one likes, but one can only express opposition at one's peril. In a democratic system of propaganda no one is punished (in theory) for objecting to official dogma. In fact, dissidence is encouraged. What this system attempts to do is to fix the limits of possible thought: supporters of official doctrine at one end, and the critics—vigorous, courageous, and much admired for their independence of judgment—at the other. The hawks and the doves. But we discover that all share certain tacit assumptions, and that it is these assumptions that are really crucial. No doubt a propaganda system is more effective when its doctrines are insinuated rather than asserted, when it sets the bounds for possible thought rather than simply imposing a clear and easily identifiable doctrine that one must parrot—or suffer the consequences. The more vigorous the debate, the more effectively the basic doctrines of the propaganda system, tacitly assumed on all sides, are instilled. Hence the elaborate pretense that the press is a critical dissenting force—maybe even too critical for the health of democracy—when in fact it is almost entirely subservient to the basic principles of the ideological system: in this case, the principle of the right of intervention, the unique right of the United States to serve as global judge and executioner. It is quite a marvelous system of indoctrination.

Here is still another example along the same lines. Look at this quotation from the *Washington Post*, a paper that is often regarded as the most consistent critic of the war among the national media. This is from an editorial of April 30, 1975, titled "Deliverance":

> For if much of the actual conduct of Vietnam policy over the years was wrong and misguided—even tragic—it cannot be denied that some part of the purpose of that policy was right and defensible. Specifically, it was right to hope that the people of South Vietnam would be able to decide on their own form of government and social order. The American public is entitled, indeed obligated, to explore how good impulses came to be transmuted into bad policy, but we cannot afford to cast out all remembrance of that earlier impulse.

What were the "good impulses"? When precisely did the United States try to help the South Vietnamese choose their own form of government and social order? As soon as such questions are posed, the absurdity becomes evident. From the moment that the American-backed French effort to destroy the major nationalist movement in Vietnam collapsed, the United

States was consciously and knowingly opposed to the organized political forces within South Vietnam, and resorted to
increasing violence when these political forces could not be
crushed. But these facts, easily documented, must be sup-
pressed. The liberal press cannot question the basic doctrine of
the state religion, that the United States is benevolent, even
though often misguided in its innocence, that it labors to permit free choice, even though at times some mistakes are committed in the exuberance of its programs of international
goodwill. We must believe that we "Americans" are always
good, though, to be sure, fallible:

> For the fundamental "lesson" of Vietnam surely is not that
> we as a people are intrinsically bad, but rather that we are ca-
> pable of error—and on a gigantic scale. . . .

Note the rhetoric: "we as a people" are not intrinsically bad,
even if we are capable of error. Was it "we as a people" who decided to conduct the war in Vietnam? Or was it something that
had rather more to do with our political leaders and the social
institutions they serve? To pose such a question is of course illegitimate, according to the dogmas of the state religion, because that raises the question of the institutional sources of
power, and such questions are only considered by irrational ex-
tremists who must be excluded from debate (we can raise such
questions with regard to other societies, of course, but not the
United States).

It is not out of pessimism that I believe in the effectiveness
of such techniques of legitimation of U.S. interventions, as a
basis for future actions. One must not forget that while the U.S.

government suffered a setback in Vietnam, it succeeded only too well in Indonesia, in Chile, in Brazil, and in many other places during the same period.

The resources of imperialist ideology are quite vast. It tolerates—indeed, encourages—a variety of forms of opposition, such as those I have just illustrated. It is permissible to criticize the lapses of the intellectuals and of government advisers, and even to accuse them of an abstract desire for "domination," again a socially neutral category, not linked in any way to concrete social and economic structures. But to relate that abstract "desire for domination" to the employment of force by the United States government in order to preserve a certain system of world order, specifically, to ensure that the countries of the world remain open insofar as possible to exploitation by U.S.-based corporations—that is extremely impolite, that is to argue in an unacceptable way.

In the same way, the respectable members of the academic world must ignore the substantial documentation concerning the principles that guide U.S. foreign policy, and its concern to create a global economic order that conforms to the needs of the U.S. economy and its masters. I'm referring, for example, to the crucial documentation contained in the *Pentagon Papers*, covering the late 1940s and early 1950s, when the basic policies were clearly set, or the documents on global planning for the postwar period produced in the early 1940s by the War-Peace Studies groups of the Council on Foreign Relations, to mention only two significant examples. Quite generally, the question of the influence of corporations on foreign policy, or the economic factors in policy formation, are reserved for the barest mention in a footnote in respectable studies of the formation of policy, a

fact that has been occasionally studied, and is easily documented when studied.

RONAT: To reveal the profits of "philanthrophy," that is hardly
in good taste.

In fact, all that you have been saying suggests to me a curious convergence, in the form of a provisional conclusion, that
goes back to the initial question: What can the links be between
a theory of ideology and the concepts of your linguistic theory,
generative grammar?

The imperialist ideology, you say, can readily tolerate a quite
large number of contradictions, infractions, and criticisms—
all these remain acceptable, *except one:* to reveal the economic
motives. You have a situation of the same kind in generative
poetics. I am thinking of the analysis which Halle and Keyser [8]
proposed for English iambic pentameter.

The verse has a structure of alternating strong and weak
stresses:

$$WS, WS, WS, WS, WS,$$
(where W = weak and S = strong)

But if one studies the corpus of English poetry, one finds an
enormous number of contradictions to the meter, of "infractions" of the dominant schema, and these verses are not only
acceptable but often even the most beautiful. *One thing only is
forbidden:* to make a weak position in the meter (in the abstract
verse schema) correspond to a stressed vowel surrounded by
two unstressed vowels. (Halle and Keyser's concept of "maxi-
mum stress.")

The observation of this kind of forbidden statement in the media permits the hope that the theory of ideology can reveal the objective laws which underlie political discourse; but for the time being all that is only a metaphor.

Notes

1. In *Liberation* (January 1973).
2. See *Ramparts* (April 1973); *Social Policy* (September 1973).
3. This appeared in the last number of that journal, which was not able to find financial support and no longer exists. *Ramparts* (August 1975).
4. See Dave Dellinger, *More Power Than We Know* (New York: Doubleday, 1975); and N. Chomsky, introduction to *Cointelpro*, ed. N. Blackstock (New York: Vintage Books, 1976), for some examples.
5. *The New Industrial State* (New York: Signet Books, 1967), 335.
6. Manuel Uribe, *Le livre noir de l'intervention américaine au Chile* (Paris: Le Seuil, 1974).
7. Jean Pierre Faye, *Le Portugal d'Otelo: La révolution dans le labyrinthe* (Paris: J.-C. Lattès, 1976), contains an analysis of the reporting on the November 1975 coup in Portugal.
8. Morris Halle and S. Jay Keyser, *English Stress, Its Form, Its Growth and Its Role in Verse* (New York: Harper & Row, 1971), and "Chaucer and the Study of Prosody," *College English* 28 (1966): 187–219.

3.

A Philosophy of Language

Noam Chomsky

MITSOU RONAT: Your linguistic discoveries have led you to take positions in philosophy of language and in what is called "philosophy of knowledge." In particular, in your last book (*Reflections on Language*), you were induced to determine the limits of what is *knowable in thought*; as a result, the reflections on language became transformed virtually into a philosophy of science.

NOAM CHOMSKY: Of course, it is not the study of language that determines what is to count as a scientific approach; but in fact this study provides a useful model to which one can refer in the investigation of human knowledge.

In the case of language, one must explain how an individual, presented with quite limited data, develops an extremely rich system of knowledge. The child, placed in a linguistic community, is presented with a set of sentences that is limited and often imperfect, fragmented, and so on. In spite of this, in a very short time he succeeds in "constructing," in internalizing the grammar of his language, developing knowledge that is very complex, that cannot be derived by induction or abstraction from what is given in experience. We conclude that the internalized knowledge must be limited very narrowly by some biological property. Whenever we encounter a similar situation, where knowledge is constructed from limited and imperfect data in a manner that is uniform and homogeneous among all individuals, we can conclude that a set of initial constraints plays a significant role in determining the cognitive system which is constructed by the mind.

We find ourselves faced with what may seem a paradox, though it is in fact not a paradox at all: where rich and complex knowledge can be constructed in a uniform way, as in the case of knowledge of language, there must exist constraints, limitations imposed by biological endowment on the cognitive systems that can be developed by the mind. The scope of attainable knowledge is linked in a fundamental way with its limits.

RONAT: If all kinds of grammatical rules were possible, then the acquisition of these rules would become impossible; if all combinations of phonemes were possible, there would no longer be language. The study of language shows, on the contrary, to what extent the sequential combinations of words, of phonemes, are limited, that these combinations form only a small subset of the set of imaginable combinations. Linguistics must render explicit the rules which limit these combinations. But on the basis of these limits one obtains an infinity of language forms . . .

CHOMSKY: If sharp limits on attainable knowledge did not exist, we could never have such extensive knowledge as that of language. For the simple reason that without these prior limitations, we could construct an enormous number of possible systems of knowledge, each compatible with what is given in experience. So the uniform attainment of some specific system of knowledge that extends far beyond experience would be impossible: we might adopt different cognitive systems, with no possibility of determining which of these systems is in fact the right one. If we have a considerable number of theories that are comparable in credibility, that is virtually the same as having no theory at all.

Let us suppose that we discover a domain of intelligence where human beings excel. If someone has developed a rich explanatory theory in spite of the limitations of available evidence, it is legitimate to ask what the general procedure is that has permitted this move from experience to knowledge—what is the system of constraints that has made possible such an intellectual leap.

The history of science might provide some relevant examples. At certain times, rich scientific theories have been constructed on the basis of limited data, theories that were intelligible to others, consisting of propositions linked in some manner to the nature of human intelligence. Given such cases, we might try to discover the initial constraints that characterize these theories. That leads us back to posing the question: What is the "universal grammar" for intelligible theories; what is the set of biologically given constraints?

Suppose we can answer this question—in principle that might be possible. Then, the constraints being given, we can inquire into the kinds of theories that can in principle be attained. This amounts to the same thing as when we ask, in the case of language: Given a theory of universal grammar, what types of languages are in principle possible?

Let us refer to the class of theories made available by the biological constraints as *accessible theories*. It may be that this class will not be homogeneous, that there will be degrees of accessibility, accessibility relative to other theories, etc. In other words, the theory of accessibility may be more or less structured. The "universal grammar" for theory construction is then a theory of the structure of accessible theories. If this "universal grammar" is part of the biological endowment of a person, then given appropriate evidence, the person will, in some cases at least, have certain accessible theories available. Admittedly, I'm simplifying greatly.

Consider then the class of *true* theories. We can imagine that such a class exists, expressed, let us say, in some notation available to us. Then we can ask: What is the *intersection* of the class of accessible theories and the class of true theories, that is to say, which theories belong at the same time to the class of accessible theories and to the class of true theories? (Or we can raise more complex questions about degree of accessibility and relative accessibility.) Where such an intersection exists, a human being can attain real knowledge. And conversely, he cannot attain real knowledge beyond that intersection.

Of course, this is on the assumption that the human mind is part of nature, that it is a biological system like others, perhaps more intricate and complex than others that we know about but a biological system nevertheless, with its potential scope and its intrinsic limits determined by the very factors that provide its scope. Human reason, on this view, is not the universal instrument that Descartes took it to be but rather a specific biological system.

RONAT: We come back again to the idea according to which scientific activity is not possible except within the biological limits of the human being . . .

CHOMSKY: But notice that there is no particular biological reason why such an intersection should exist. The capacity to invent nuclear physics provides an organism with no selectional advantage and was not a factor in human evolution, it is reasonable to assume. The ability to solve algebra problems is not a factor in differential reproduction. There is, to my knowledge, no credible version of the view that these special capacities are somehow continuous with practical abilities, toolmaking, and the like—which is not to deny, of course, that these special capacities developed for unknown reasons as a concomitant of evolution of the brain that may have been subject to selectional pressures.

In a sense, the existence of an intersection of the class of accessible theories and the class of true theories is a kind of biological miracle. It seems that this miracle took place at least in one domain, namely, physics, and the natural sciences that one might think of loosely as a kind of "extension" of physics: chemistry, biochemistry, molecular biology. In these domains, progress has been extremely rapid on the basis of limited data, and in a manner intelligible to others. Perhaps we are confronted here with a unique episode in human history: there is nothing to lead one to believe that we are a universal organism.

Rather, we are subject to biological limitations with respect to the theories we can devise and comprehend, and we are fortunate to have these limitations, for otherwise we could not construct rich systems of knowledge and understanding at all. But these limitations may well exclude domains about which we would like very much to know something. That's too bad. Perhaps there is another organism with a differently organized intelligence that would be capable of what we are not. This is, as a first approximation, a reasonable one in my opinion, a way to think about the question of acquisition of conscious knowledge.

Going a step further, it is not unimaginable that a particular organism might come to examine its *own* system of acquiring knowledge; it might thus be able to determine the class of intelligible theories which it can attain. I don't see any contradiction in that. A theory which is found to be unintelligible, an "inaccessible theory" in the sense just given, does not thereby become intelligible or accessible.

It would simply be identified. And if in some domain of thought the accessible theories turn out to be remote from the true theories, that's too bad. Then human beings can, at best, develop a kind of intellectual technology, which for inexplicable reasons predicts certain things in these domains. But they won't truly *understand* why the technology is working. They will not possess an intelligible theory in the sense that an interesting science is intelligible. Their theories, though perhaps effective, will be intellectually unsatisfying.

Looking at the history of human intellectual endeavor from this point of view, we find curious things, surprising things. In mathematics certain areas seem to correspond to exceptional human aptitudes: number theory, spatial intuition. Pursuit of these intuitions determined the main line of progress in mathematics, until the end of the nineteenth century, at least. Apparently our mind is capable of handling the abstract properties of number systems, abstract geometry, and the mathematics of the continuum. These are not the absolute limits, but it is probable that we are confined to certain branches of science and mathematics.

Presumably, all that I have just said would be rejected by a strict empiricist, or even regarded as senseless.

RONAT: That is to say by someone who believes in the proposition according to which man proceeds by induction and generalization in the acquisition of knowledge, starting from "empty" or "blank" minds, without a priori biological limitations. Within that framework, knowledge is no more determined by the structure of the mind than is the form of a design by the wax tablet . . .

CHOMSKY: Yes. These empiricist hypotheses have very little plausibility, in my opinion; it does not seem possible to account for the development of commonsense understanding of the physical and social world, or science, in terms of processes of induction, generalization, abstraction, and so on. There is no such direct path from data that are given to intelligible theories.

The same is true in other domains, music, for example. After all, you can always imagine innumerable musical systems, most of which will seem to the human ear to be just noise. There too, biological factors determine the class of possible musical systems for human beings, though what exactly this class may be is an open and currently debated question.

In this case as well, no direct functional explanation seems available. Musical ability is not a factor in reproduction. Music does not improve material well-being, does not permit one to function better in society, etc. Quite simply, it responds to the human need for aesthetic expression. If we study human nature in a proper way, we may discover that certain musical systems correspond to that need, while others do not.

RONAT: Among those fields in which the scientific approach has not made any progress in two thousand years you list the study of human behavior.

CHOMSKY: Behavior, yes, that is one such case. The basic questions have been posed since the beginning of historical memory: the question of causation of behavior seems simple enough to pose, but virtually no theoretical progress has been made in answering it. One might formulate the basic question as follows: Consider a function of certain variables such that, given the values of the variables, the function will give us the behavior that results under the conditions specified by these values, or perhaps some distribution over possible behaviors. But no such function has been seriously proposed, even to a weak approximation, and the question has remained without issue. In fact, we don't know of any reasonable way to approach the problem. It is conceivable that this persistent failure is to be explained on the grounds that the true theory of behavior is beyond our cognitive reach. Therefore we can make no progress. It would be as if we tried to teach a monkey to appreciate Bach. A waste of time . . .

RONAT: Then the question of behavior would be different from the question of syntax: that too had never been posed before the development of generative grammar.

CHOMSKY: But in this case, once the question is posed, everyone comes up with answers that are similar or comparable. When certain questions are posed, sometimes the answer is impossible to imagine, sometimes answers begin to appear quite widely. And when an answer is proposed, those who have an adequate understanding of the question will also regard the answer as intelligible. It is often the case that a question cannot yet properly be posed, or posed with the requisite degree of sophistication; but then it can sometimes be posed properly, and still seem to lie beyond our intellectual grasp.

Another analogue to the case of language, perhaps, is our comprehension of the social structures in which we live. We have all sorts of tacit and complex knowledge concerning our relations to other people. Perhaps we have a sort of "universal grammar" of possible forms of social interaction, and it is this system which helps us to organize intuitively our imperfect perceptions of social reality, though it does not follow necessarily that we are capable of developing conscious theories in this domain through the exercise of our "science-forming faculties." If we succeed in finding our place within our society, that is perhaps because these societies have a structure that we are prepared to seek out. With a little imagination we could devise an artificial society in which no one could ever find his place . . .

RONAT: Then you can compare the failure of artificial languages with the failure of utopian societies?

CHOMSKY: Perhaps. One cannot learn an artificial language constructed to violate universal grammar as readily as one learns a natural language, simply by being immersed in it. At most, one might conceive of such a language as a game, a puzzle . . . In the same way we can imagine a society in which no one could survive as a social being because it does not correspond to biologically determined perceptions and human social needs. For historical reasons, existing societies might have such properties, leading to various forms of pathology.

Any serious social science or theory of social change must be founded on some concept of human nature. A theorist of classical liberalism such as Adam Smith begins by affirming that human nature is defined by a propensity to truck and barter, to exchange goods: that assumption accords very well with the social order he defends. If you accept that premise (which is hardly credible), it turns out that human nature conforms to an idealized early capitalist society, without monopoly, without state intervention, and without social control of production.

If, on the contrary, you believe with Marx or the French and German Romantics that only social cooperation permits the full development of human powers, you will then have a very different picture of a desirable society. There is always some conception of human nature, implicit or explicit, underlying a doctrine of social order or social change.

RONAT: To what degree can your discoveries about language and your definitions of fields of knowledge lead to the emergence of new philosophic questions? To which philosophy do you feel closest?

CHOMSKY: In relation to the questions we have just been discussing, the philosopher to whom I feel closest and whom I'm almost paraphrasing is Charles Sanders Peirce. He proposed an interesting outline, very far from complete, of what he called "abduction" . . .

RONAT: Abduction is, I believe, a form of inference which does not depend solely on a priori principles (like deduction), nor solely on experimental observation (like induction). But that aspect of Peirce is very little known in France.

CHOMSKY: Or here in the United States either. Peirce argued that to account for the growth of knowledge, one must assume that "man's mind has a natural adaptation to imagining correct theories of some kinds," some principle of "abduction" which "puts a limit on admissible hypothesis," a kind of "instinct," developed in the course of evolution. Peirce's ideas on abduction were rather vague, and his suggestion that biologically given structure plays a basic role in the selection of scientific hypotheses seems to have had very little influence. To my knowledge, almost no one has tried to develop these ideas further, although similar notions have been developed independently on various occasions. Peirce has had an enormous influence, but not for this particular reason.

RONAT: More in semiology . . .

CHOMSKY: Yes, in that general area. His ideas on abduction developed Kantian ideas to which recent Anglo-American philosophy has not been very receptive. As far as I know, his approach in epistemology has never been followed up, even though there has been much criticism of inductivist approaches—Popper, for example.

Russell, for his part, was much preoccupied in his later work (*Human Knowledge*) with the inadequacy of the empiricist approach to the acquisition of knowledge. But this book has generally been ignored. He proposed various principles of *non-demonstrative inference* with the aim of accounting for the knowledge which in reality we possess.

RONAT: Non-demonstrative inference differs from the deductions of mathematical logic to the degree where, in spite of the truth of the premises and the rigorous character of the reasoning, the truth of the conclusions is not guaranteed; they are only rendered *probable*. Is that it?

CHOMSKY: In substance, yes: one might say that his approach here was Kantian to a certain degree, but with fundamental differences. In some way, Russell remained an empiricist. His principles of non-demonstrative inference are *added* one by one to the fundamental principle of induction and do not offer a radical change in perspective. But the problem is not quantitative, it is qualitative. The principles of non-demonstrative inference do not fulfill the need. I believe a radically different approach is necessary, which takes a starting point that is quite remote from empiricist presuppositions. This is true not only for scientific knowledge, where it is generally accepted today, but also for what we can call the constructions of "common-sense understanding," that is, for our ordinary notions concerning the nature of the physical and social world, our intuitive comprehension of human actions, their ends, their reasons, and their causes, etc.

These are very important issues, which would demand much more analysis than I can give here. But to return to your question, a great deal of the work of contemporary philosophers on language and the nature of scientific research has been very stimulating for me. My own work, from the very beginning, was greatly influenced by developments in philosophy (as the published acknowledgments of indebtedness indicate; particularly, to Nelson Goodman and W.V. Quine). And that continues to be true. To mention only a few examples, the work of John Austin on speech acts proved very fruitful, as well as that of Paul Grice on the logic of conversation. At present very interesting work is being pursued on the theory of meaning along various lines. One can cite the contributions of Saul Kripke, Hilary Putnam, Jerrold Katz, Michael Dummett, Julius Moravcsik, Donald Davidson, and many others. Certain of the work on model-theoretic semantics—the study of "truth in possible worlds"—seems promising. In particular, I would mention the work of Jaakko Hintikka and his colleagues, which deals with questions that are central to quite a range of topics in syntax and semantics of natural languages, particularly with regard to quantification. Such work has also been extended to pragmatics, that is to the study of the manner in which language is used to accomplish certain human ends; for example, the work of the Israeli philosopher Asa Kasher. As these few brief references indicate, this work is being done on an international scale and is not just Anglo-American.

I should also mention work on history and philosophy of

science, which has begun to furnish a richer and more exact understanding of the manner in which ideas develop and take root in the natural sciences. This work—for example, that of Thomas Kuhn or Imre Lakatós—has gone well beyond the often artificial models of verification and falsification, which were prevalent for a long time and which exercised a dubious influence on the "soft sciences," as the latter did not rest on the foundations of a healthy intellectual tradition that could guide their development. It is useful, in my opinion, for people working in these fields to become familiar with ways in which the natural sciences have been able to progress; in particular, to recognize how, at critical moments of their development, they have been guided by radical idealization, a concern for depth of insight and explanatory power rather than by a concern to accommodate "all the facts"—a notion that approaches meaninglessness—even at times disregarding apparent counterexamples in the hope (which at times has proven justified only after many years or even centuries) that subsequent insights would explain them. These are useful lessons that have been obscured in much of the discussion about epistemology and the philosophy of science.

RONAT: What do you think of European philosophers, of the French in particular?

CHOMSKY: Outside of Anglo-American philosophy, I do not know enough about contemporary philosophers to discuss them at all seriously.

RONAT: Have you ever met any French Marxist philosophers?

CHOMSKY: Rarely. Here some distinctions are necessary. Contemporary Marxist philosophy has been linked in large part to Leninist doctrine, at least until recently. European Marxism after World War I developed unfortunate tendencies, in my opinion: the tendencies associated with Bolshevism, which has always seemed to me an authoritarian and reactionary current. The latter became dominant within the European Marxist tradition after the Russian Revolution. But much more to my taste, at least, are quite different tendencies, for example, that range of opinion that extends roughly from Rosa Luxemburg and the Dutch Marxist Anton Pannekoek and Paul Mattick to the anarcho-syndicalist Rudolf Rocker and others.

These thinkers have not contributed to philosophy in the sense of our discussion; but they have much to say about society, about social change, and the fundamental problems of human life. Though not about problems of the sort that we have been discussing, for example.

Marxism itself has become too often a sort of church, a theology.

Of course, I'm generalizing far too much. Work of value has been done by those who consider themselves Marxists. But up to a certain point this criticism is justified, I'm afraid. In any case, I do not believe that Marxist philosophy, of whatever tendency, has made a substantial contribution to the kind of questions we have been discussing.

For the rest, what I know has not impressed me greatly and has not encouraged me to seek to know more.

RONAT: But you met Michel Foucault, I believe, during a television broadcast in Amsterdam?

CHOMSKY: Yes, and we had some very good discussions before and during the broadcast. On Dutch television, we spoke for several hours, he in French and I in English; I don't know what the Dutch television viewers made of all that. We found ourselves in at least partial agreement, it seemed to me, on the question of "human nature," and perhaps not as much on politics (the two basic points about which Fons Elders interviewed us).

As far as the concept of human nature and its relation to scientific progress was concerned, it seemed that we were "climbing the same mountain, starting from opposite directions," to repeat a simile which Elders suggested. In my view, scientific creativity depends on two facts: on the one hand, on an intrinsic property of mind, and on the other, on a combination of social and intellectual conditions. There is no question of choosing between these. In order to understand a scientific discovery, it is necessary to understand the interaction between these factors. But personally I am more interested in the first, while Foucault stresses the second.

Foucault considers the scientific knowledge of a given epoch to be like a *grid* of social and intellectual conditions, like a system the rules of which permit the creation of new knowledge. In his view, if I understand him correctly, human knowledge is transformed due to social conditions and social struggles, with one grid replacing the other, thus bringing new possibilities to science. He is, I believe, skeptical about the possibility or the legitimacy of an attempt to place important sources of human knowledge within the human mind, conceived in an ahistorical manner.

His position also involves a different usage of the term *creativity*. When I speak of creativity in this context, I am not making a value judgment: creativity is an aspect of the ordinary and daily use of language and of human action in general. However, when Foucault speaks of creativity he is thinking more of the achievements of a Newton, for example—although he stresses the common social and intellectual base for the creations of scientific imagination, rather than the achievements of an individual genius—that is to say, he is thinking of the conditions for radical innovation. His use of the term is a more normal one than mine. But even if contemporary science may find some solution to problems relating to ordinary, normal creativity—and I am rather skeptical even about this—still it cannot hope, certainly, to be able to come to grips with true creativity in the more usual sense of the word, or say, to foresee the achievements of great artists or the future discoveries of science. That seems a hopeless quest. In my opinion, the sense in which I am speaking of "normal creativity" is not unlike what Descartes had in mind when he made the distinction between a human being and a parrot. In the historical perspective of Foucault, one no longer seeks to identify the innovators and their specific achievement or the obstacles which stand in the way of the emergence of truth, but to determine how knowledge, as a system independent of individuals, modifies its own rules of formation.

RONAT: In defining the knowledge of an epoch as a grid or system, doesn't Foucault draw near to structuralist thought, which also conceives of language as a system?

CHOMSKY: To reply properly it would be necessary to study this matter in depth. In any case, while I have been speaking of

the limitations imposed on a class of accessible theories—
linked to the limitations of the human mind that permit the
construction of rich theories in the first place—he is more interested in the proliferation of theoretical possibilities resulting from the diversity of social conditions within which human
intelligence can flourish.

RONAT: In the same way, structuralist linguistics stresses the
differences between languages.

CHOMSKY: I have to be cautious in response, because the expression "structural linguistics" can cover a great variety of positions. It is certainly true that American "neo-Bloomfieldian"
linguists, who sometimes call themselves "structuralists," have
been impressed above all by the diversity of languages, and that
some of them, like Martin Joos, have gone so far as to declare, as
a general proposition of linguistic science, that languages can
differ from one another in an arbitrary manner. When they
speak of "universals," this involves a characterization of a very
limited nature, perhaps some statistical observations. On the
other hand, such a characterization would be very wide of its
mark in the case of other schools of structural linguistics; for
example, the work of Roman Jakobson, who has always been
concerned with linguistic universals which narrowly constrain
the class of possible languages, especially in phonology.

   As far as Foucault is concerned, as I've said, he seems skeptical about the possibility of developing a concept of "human
nature" that is independent of social and historical conditions,
as a well-defined biological concept. I don't believe that he
would characterize his own approach as "structuralist." I don't

share his skepticism. I would be in agreement with him in saying that human nature is not as yet within the range of science. Up to the present, it has escaped the reach of scientific inquiry; but I believe that in specific domains such as the study of language, we can begin to formulate a significant concept of "human nature," in its intellectual and cognitive aspects. In any case, I would not hesitate to consider the faculty of language as part of human nature.

RONAT: Did you and Foucault speak of the Port-Royal *Grammaire Générale?*

CHOMSKY: More precisely, about my relationship to the work on the history of ideas. There are a number of misunderstandings on this subject.

These questions can be approached in various ways. My approach to the early modern rationalist tradition, for example, is not that of a historian of science or of philosophy. I have not attempted to reconstruct in an exhaustive manner what people thought at that time, but rather to bring to light certain important insights of the period that have been neglected, and often seriously distorted, in later scholarship, and to show how at that time certain persons had already discerned important things, perhaps without being fully aware of it. These specific intentions are spelled out quite explicitly in my book *Cartesian Linguistics*, for example.

I was interested in earlier stages of thought and speculation relating to questions of contemporary significance. And I tried to show in what ways and to what extent similar ideas were formulated, anticipations of later developments, perhaps from rather different perspectives. I think that we can often see, from our current vantage point in the progress of understanding, how a thinker of the past was groping toward certain extremely significant ideas, frequently in a very constructive and remarkable manner, and perhaps with only a partial awareness of the nature of his quest.

Let me offer an analogy. I am not proceeding in the manner of an art historian so much as that of an art lover, a person who looks for what has value to him in the seventeenth century, for example, that value deriving in large measure from the contemporary perspective with which he approaches these objects. Both types of approach are legitimate. I think it is possible to turn toward earlier stages of scientific knowledge, and by virtue of what we know today, to shed light on the significant contributions of the period in a way in which the most creative geniuses could not, because of the limitations of their time. This was the nature of my interest in Descartes, for example, and in the philosophical tradition that he influenced, and also Humboldt, who would not have considered himself a Cartesian: I was interested in his effort to make sense of the concept of free creativity based on a system of internalized rules, an idea that has certain roots in Cartesian thought, I believe.

The kind of approach I was taking has been criticized, but not on any rational grounds, so far as I can see. Perhaps I should have discussed the nature and legitimacy of such an approach in more detail, though it seemed to me (and still seems to me) obvious. What I have been saying is quite familiar in the history of science. For example, Dijksterhuis, in his major work on the origins of classical mechanics, points out, with reference to Newton, that "Properly speaking, the whole system can only be understood in the light of the subsequent development of the science."[1] Suppose that the insights of classical mechanics had been lost, and there had been a reversion to something more akin to "natural history"—the accumulation and organization of large amounts of data and phenomenal observations, perhaps a kind of Babylonian astronomy (though even this reference is probably unfair). Then suppose that in some new phase of science, questions similar to those of the period of classical mechanics had reemerged. It would then have been entirely appropriate, quite important in fact, to try to discover significant insights of an earlier period and to determine in what ways they were anticipations of current work, perhaps to be understood properly in the light of subsequent developments. This it seems to me is more or less what happened in the study of language and mind, and I think it is quite interesting to recover insights that have long been neglected, approaching earlier work (which has often been grossly misrepresented, as I showed) from the standpoint of current interests and trying to see how questions discussed in an earlier period can be understood, and sometimes reinterpreted, in the light of more recent understanding, knowledge, and technique. This is a legitimate approach, not to be confused with efforts (like those of Dijksterhuis in physics) to reconstruct exactly how the issues appeared and how ideas were constructed at an earlier time. Of course, one must be careful not to falsify earlier discussion, but I am aware of no critical analysis of my work that shows this to be the case. There has, I am sorry to say, been a good deal of outright misrepresentation of what I wrote, in what is called "the scholarly literature," and I have been surprised to find sharp criticism of my alleged views even on topics that I did not discuss at all. I have commented occasionally on some of these falsifications, as have others, but by no means exhaustively, and I won't pursue it here.

Any person engaged in intellectual work can do the same thing with himself: you can try to reconsider what you understood twenty years ago, and thus see in what direction, in a confused manner, you were striving to go, toward what goal that perhaps became clear and intelligible only much later . . .

RONAT: What were the political disagreements between you and Foucault?

CHOMSKY: For my part, I would distinguish two intellectual tasks. One is to imagine a future society that conforms to the exigencies of human nature, as best we understand them; the other, to analyze the nature of power and oppression in our present societies. For him, if I understand him rightly, what we can imagine now is nothing but a product of the bourgeois society of the modern period: the notions of justice or of "realization of the human essence" are only the inventions of our civilization and result from our class system. The concept of justice is thus reduced to a pretext advanced by a class that has or wants to have access to power. The task of a reformer or revolutionary is to gain power, not to bring about a more just society. Questions of abstract justice are not posed, and perhaps cannot even be posed intelligibly. Foucault says, again if I understand him correctly, that one engages in the class struggle to win, not because that will lead to a more just society. In this respect I have a very different opinion. A social struggle, in my view, can only be justified if it is supported by an argument—

even if it is an indirect argument based on questions of fact and value that are not well understood—which purports to show that the consequences of this struggle will be beneficial for human beings and will bring about a more decent society. Let us take the case of violence. I am not a committed pacifist, and thus do not say that it is wrong to use violence in all circumstances, say in self-defense. But any recourse to violence must be justified, perhaps by an argument that it is necessary to remedy injustice. If a revolutionary victory of the proletariat were to lead to putting the rest of the world into crematoria, then the class struggle is not justified. It can only be justified by an argument that it will bring an end to class oppression, and do so in a way that accords with fundamental human rights. Complicated questions arise here, no doubt, but they should be faced. We were in apparent disagreement, because where I was speaking of justice, he was speaking of power. At least, that is how the difference between our points of view appeared to me.

Notes

1. E.J. Dijksterhuis, *The Mechanization of the World Picture* (London: Oxford University Press, 1961), 466.

4.

Truth and Power

Michel Foucault

QUESTION: Could you briefly outline the route that led you from your work on madness in the Classical age to the study of criminality and delinquency?

MICHEL FOUCAULT: When I was studying during the early fifties, one of the great problems that arose was that of the political status of science and the ideological functions it could serve. It wasn't exactly the Lysenko business that dominated everything, but I believe that around that sordid affair—which had long remained buried and carefully hidden—a whole number of interesting questions were provoked. These can all be summed up in two words: power and knowledge. I believe I wrote *Madness and Civilization* to some extent within the horizon of these questions. For me, it was a matter of saying this: If, concerning a science like theoretical physics or organic chemistry, one poses the problem of its relations with the political and economic structures of society, isn't one posing an excessively complicated question? Doesn't this set the threshold of possible explanations impossibly high? But, on the other hand, if one takes a form of knowledge *(savoir)* like psychiatry, won't the question be much easier to resolve, since the epistemological profile of psychiatry is a low one and psychiatric practice is linked with a whole range of institutions, economic requirements, and political issues of social regulation? Couldn't the interweaving of effects of power and knowledge be grasped with greater certainty in the case of a science as "dubious" as psychiatry? It was this same question which I wanted to pose concerning medicine in *The Birth of the Clinic*: medicine certainly has a much more solid scientific armature than psychiatry, but it too is profoundly enmeshed in social structures. What rather threw me at the time was the fact that the question I was posing totally failed to interest those to whom I addressed it. They regarded it as a problem that was politically unimportant and epistemologically vulgar.

I think there were three reasons for this. The first is that, for Marxist intellectuals in France (and there they were playing the role prescribed for them by the PCF), the problem consisted in gaining for themselves the recognition of the university institutions and establishment. Consequently, they found it necessary to pose the same theoretical questions as the academic establishment, to deal with the same problems and topics: "We may be Marxists, but for all that we are not strangers to your preoccupations, rather, we are the only ones able to provide new solutions for your old concerns." Marxism sought to win acceptance as a renewal of the liberal university tradition—just as, more broadly, during the same period the communists presented themselves as the only people capable of taking over and reinvigorating the nationalist tradition. Hence, in the field we are concerned with here, it followed that they wanted to take up the "noblest," most academic problems in the history of the sciences: mathematics and physics, in short the themes valorized by Pierre Maurice Marie Duhem, Edmund Husserl, and Alexandre Koyré. Medicine and psychiatry didn't seem to them to be very noble or serious matters, nor to stand on the same level as the great forms of classical rationalism.

The second reason is that post-Stalinist Stalinism, by excluding from Marxist discourse everything that wasn't a frightened repetition of the already said, would not permit the broaching of uncharted domains. There were no ready-made concepts, no approved terms of vocabulary available for questions like the power effects of psychiatry or the political function of medicine, whereas on the contrary innumerable exchanges between Marxists and academics, from Marx via Engels and Lenin down to the present, had nourished a whole tradition of discourse on "science," in the nineteenth-century sense of that term. The price Marxists paid for their fidelity to the old positivism was a radical deafness to a whole series of questions posed by science.

Finally, there is perhaps a third reason, but I can't be absolutely sure that it played a part. I wonder nevertheless whether, among intellectuals in or close to the PCF, there wasn't a refusal to pose the problem of internment, of the political use of psychiatry, and, in a more general sense, of the disciplinary grid of society. No doubt, little was then known in 1955–60 of the real extent of the gulag, but I believe that many sensed it, in any case many had a feeling that it was better not to talk about those things—it was a danger zone, marked by warning signs. Of course, it's difficult in retrospect to judge people's degree of awareness. But, in any case, you well know how easily the Party leadership—which knew everything, of course—could circulate instructions preventing people from speaking about this or that, or precluding this or that line of research. At any rate, if the question of Pavlovian psychiatry did get discussed among a few doctors close to the PCF, psychiatric politics and psychiatry as politics were hardly considered to be respectable topics.

What I myself tried to do in this domain was met with a great silence among the French intellectual Left. And it was only around 1968, and in spite of the Marxist tradition and the PCF, that all these questions came to assume their political significance, with a sharpness I had never envisaged, showing how timid and hesitant those early books of mine had still been. Without the political opening created during those years, I would surely never have had the courage to take up these problems again and pursue my research in the direction of penal theory, prisons, and disciplines.

QUESTION: So there is a certain "discontinuity" in your theoretical trajectory. Incidentally, what do you think today about this concept of discontinuity, on the basis of which you have been all too rapidly and readily labeled as a "structuralist" historian?

FOUCAULT: This business about discontinuity has always rather bewildered me. In the new edition of the _Petit Larousse_ it says: "Foucault: a philosopher who founds his theory of history on discontinuity." That leaves me flabbergasted. No doubt, I didn't make myself sufficiently clear in *The Order of Things*, though I said a good deal there about this question. It seemed to me that in certain empirical forms of knowledge like biology, political economy, psychiatry, medicine, and so on, the rhythm of transformation doesn't follow the smooth, continuist schemas of development which are normally accepted. The great biological image of a progressive maturation of science still underpins a good many historical analyses; it does not seem to me to be pertinent to history. In a science like medicine, for example, up to the end of the eighteenth century one has a certain type of discourse whose gradual transformation, within a period of twenty-five or thirty years, broke not only with the "true" propositions it had hitherto been possible to formulate but also, more profoundly, with the ways of speaking and seeing, the whole ensemble of practices which served as supports for medical knowledge. These are not simply new discoveries; there is a whole new "regime" in discourse and forms of knowledge. And all this happens in the space of a few years. This is something that is undeniable, once one has looked at the texts with sufficient attention. My problem was not at all to say *"Voilà,* long live discontinuity, we are in the discontinuous and a good thing too," but to pose the question "How is it that at certain moments and in certain orders of knowledge, there are these sudden take-offs, these hastenings of evolution, these transformations which fail to correspond to the calm, continuist image that is normally accredited?" But the important thing here is not that such changes can be rapid and extensive or, rather, it is that this extent and rapidity are only the sign of something else—a modification in the rules of formation of statements which are accepted as scientifically true. Thus, it is not a change of content (refutation of old errors, recovery of old truths), nor is it a change of theoretical form (renewal of a paradigm, modification of systematic ensembles). It is a question of what *governs* statements, and the way in which they *govern* each other so as to constitute a set of propositions that are scientifically acceptable and, hence, capable of being verified or falsified by scientific procedures. In short, there is a problem of the regime, the politics of the scientific statement. At this level, it's not so much a matter of knowing what external power imposes itself on science as of what effects of power circulate among scientific statements, what constitutes, as it were, their internal regime of power, and how and why at certain moments that regime undergoes a global modification.

It was these different regimes that I tried to identify and describe in *The Order of Things*, all the while making it clear that I wasn't trying for the moment to explain them, and that it would be necessary to try to do this in a subsequent work. But what was lacking here was this problem of the "discursive regime," of the effects of power peculiar to the play of statements. I confused this too much with systematicity, theoretical form, or something like a paradigm. This same central problem of power, which at that time I had not yet properly isolated, emerges in two very different aspects at the point of junction of *Madness and Civilization* and *The Order of Things*.

QUESTION: We need, then, to locate the notion of discontinuity in its proper context. And perhaps there is another concept that is both more difficult and more central to your thought, the concept of an event. For, in relation to the event, a whole generation was long trapped in an *impasse*, in that following the works of ethnologists—some of them great ethnologists—a dichotomy was established between structures (the *thinkable*) and the event considered as the site of the irrational, the unthinkable, that which does not and cannot enter into the mechanism and play of analysis, at least in the form which this took in structuralism. In a recent discussion published in the journal *L'Homme*, three eminent anthropologists posed this question once again about the concept of event, and said: The event is what always escapes our rational grasp, the domain of "absolute contingency"; we are thinkers who analyze structures, history is no concern of ours, what could we be expected to have to say about it, and so forth. This opposition, then, between event and structure is the site and the product of a certain anthropology. I would say this has had devastating effects among historians who have finally reached the point of trying to dismiss the event and the *événementiel* as an inferior order of history dealing with trivial facts, chance occurrences, and so on. Whereas it is a fact that there are nodal problems in history which are neither a matter of trivial circumstances nor of those beautiful structures that are so orderly, intelligible, and transparent to analysis. For instance, the "great internment" you described in *Madness and Civilization* perhaps represents one of these nodes which elude the dichotomy of structure and event. Could you elaborate from our present standpoint on this renewal and reformulation of the concept of event?

FOUCAULT: One can agree that structuralism formed the most systematic effort to evacuate the concept of the event, not only from ethnology but from a whole series of other sciences and in the extreme case from history. In that sense, I don't see who could be more of an antistructuralist than myself. But the important thing is to avoid trying to do for the event what was previously done with the concept of structure. It's not a matter of locating everything on one level, that of the event, but of realizing that there are actually a whole order of levels of different types of events differing in amplitude, chronological breadth, and capacity to produce effects.

The problem is at once to distinguish among events, to differentiate the networks and levels to which they belong, and to reconstitute the lines along which they are connected and engender one another. From this follows a refusal of analyses couched in terms of the symbolic field or the domain of signifying structures, and a recourse to analyses in terms of the genealogy of relations of force, strategic developments, and tactics. Here I believe one's point of reference should not be to the great model of language [*langue*] and signs but, rather, to that of war and battle. The history that bears and determines us has the form of a war rather than that of a language—relations of power, not relations of meaning. History has no "meaning," though this is not to say that it is absurd or incoherent. On the contrary, it is intelligible and should be susceptible of analysis down to the smallest detail—but this in accordance with the intelligibility of struggles, of strategies and tactics. Neither the dialectic, as the logic of contradictions, nor semiotics, as the structure of communication, can account for the intrinsic intelligibility of conflicts. "Dialectic" is a way of evading the always open and hazardous reality of conflict by reducing it to a Hegelian skeleton, and "semiology" is a way of avoiding its violent, bloody, and lethal character by reducing it to the calm Platonic form of language and dialogue.

QUESTION: In the context of this problem of discursivity, I think one can be confident in saying that you were the first person to pose the question of power regarding discourse, and that at a time when analyses in terms of the concept or object of the "text," along with the accompanying methodology of semiology, structuralism, and so on, were the prevailing fashion. Posing for discourse the question of power means basically to ask whom discourse serves. It isn't so much a matter of analyzing discourse into its unsaid, its implicit meaning, because (as you have often repeated) discourses are transparent, they need no interpretation, no one to assign them a meaning. If one reads "texts" in a certain way, one perceives that they speak clearly to us and require no further supplementary sense or interpretation. This question of power that you have addressed to discourse naturally has particular effects and implications in relation to methodology and contemporary historical researches. Could you briefly situate within your work this question you have posed—if indeed it's true that you have posed it?

FOUCAULT: I don't think I was the first to pose the question. On the contrary, I'm struck by the difficulty I had in formulating it. When I think back now, I ask myself what else it was that I was talking about in *Madness and Civilization* or *The Birth of the Clinic*, but power? Yet I'm perfectly aware that I scarcely ever used the word and never had such a field of analyses at my disposal. I can say that this was an incapacity linked undoubtedly with the political situation in which we found ourselves. It is hard to see where, either on the Right or the Left, this problem of power could then have been posed. On the Right, it was posed only in terms of constitution, sovereignty, and so on, that is, in juridical terms; on the Marxist side, it was posed only in terms of the state apparatus. The way power was exercised—concretely, and in detail—with its specificity, its techniques and tactics, was something that no one attempted to ascertain; they contented themselves with denouncing it in a polemical and global fashion as it existed among the "other," in the adversary camp. Where Soviet socialist power was in question, its opponents called it totalitarianism; power in Western capitalism was denounced by the Marxists as class domination; but the mechanics of power in themselves were never analyzed. This task could only begin after 1968, that is to say, on the basis of daily struggles at grassroots level, among those whose fight was located in the fine meshes of the web of power. This was where the concrete nature of power became visible, along with the prospect that these analyses of power would prove fruitful in accounting for all that had hitherto remained outside the field of political analysis. To put it very simply, psychiatric internment, the mental normalization of individuals, and penal institutions have no doubt a fairly limited importance if one is only looking for their economic significance. On the other hand, they are undoubtedly essential to the general functioning of the wheels of power. So long as the posing of the question of power was kept subordinate to the economic instance and the system of interests this served, there was a tendency to regard these problems as of small importance.

QUESTION: So a certain kind of Marxism and a certain kind of phenomenology constituted an objective obstacle to the formulation of this problematic?

FOUCAULT: Yes, if you like, to the extent that it's true that, in our student days, people of my generation were brought up on these two forms of analysis, one in terms of the constituent subject, the other in terms of the economic in the last instance, ideology and the play of superstructures and infrastructures.

QUESTION: Still within this methodological context, how would you situate the genealogical approach? As a questioning of the conditions of possibility, modalities, and constitution of the "objects" and domains you have successively analyzed, what makes it necessary?

FOUCAULT: I wanted to see how these problems of constitution could be resolved within a historical framework, instead of referring them back to a constituent object (madness, criminality, or whatever). But this historical contextualization needed to be something more than the simple relativization of the phenomenological subject. I don't believe the problem can be solved by historicizing the subject as posited by the phenomenologists, fabricating a subject that evolves through the course of history. One has to dispense with the constituent subject, to get rid of the subject itself, that's to say, to arrive at an analysis that can account for the constitution of the subject within a historical framework. And this is what I would call genealogy, that is, a form of history that can account for the constitution of knowledges, discourses, domains of objects, and so on, without having to make reference to a subject that is either transcendental in relation to the field of events or runs in its empty sameness throughout the course of history.

QUESTION: Marxist phenomenology and a certain kind of Marxism have clearly acted as a screen and an obstacle; there are two further concepts that continue today to act as a screen and an obstacle—ideology, on the one hand, and repression, on the other.

All history comes to be thought of within these categories, which serve to assign a meaning to such diverse phenomena as normalization, sexuality, and power. And, regardless of whether these two concepts are explicitly utilized, in the end one always comes back, on the one hand, to ideology—where it is easy to make the reference back to Marx—and, on the other, to repression, which is a concept often and readily employed by Freud throughout the course of his career. Hence, I would like to put forward the following suggestion: Behind these concepts and among those who (properly or improperly) employ them, there is a kind of nostalgia. Behind the concept of ideology lies the nostalgia for a quasi-transparent form of knowledge, free from all error and illusion, and behind the concept of repression is the longing for a form of power innocent of all coercion, discipline, and normalization. On the one hand, a power without a bludgeon, and, on the other, knowledge without deception. You have called these two concepts, ideology and repression, negative, "psychological," insufficiently analytical. This is particularly the case in *Discipline and Punish* where, even if there isn't an extended discussion of these concepts, there is nevertheless a kind of analysis that allows one to go beyond the traditional forms of explanation and intelligibility, which in the last (and not only the last) instance rest on the concepts of ideology and repression. Could you perhaps use this occasion to specify more explicitly your thoughts on these matters? With *Discipline and Punish,* a kind of positive history seems to be emerging, free of all the negativity and psychologism implicit in those two universal skeleton keys.

FOUCAULT: The notion of ideology appears to me to be difficult to make use of, for three reasons. The first is that, like it or not, it always stands in virtual opposition to something else that is supposed to count as truth. Now, I believe that the problem does not consist in drawing the line between that which, in a discourse, falls under the category of scientificity or truth, and that which comes under some other category; rather, it consists in seeing historically how effects of truth are produced within discourses that, in themselves, are neither true nor false. The second drawback is that the concept of ideology refers, I think necessarily, to something of the order of a subject. Third, ideology stands in a secondary position relative to something that functions as its infrastructure, as its material, economic determinant, and so on. For these three reasons, I think that this is a notion that cannot be used without circumspection.

The notion of repression is a more insidious one, or, in any event, I myself have had much more trouble in freeing myself of it insofar as it does indeed appear to correspond so well with a whole range of phenomena that belong among the effects of power. When I wrote *Madness and Civilization*, I made at least an implicit use of this notion of repression. I think indeed that I was positing the existence of a sort of living, voluble, and anxious madness that the mechanisms of power and psychiatry were supposed to have come to repress and reduce to silence. But it seems to me now that the notion of repression is quite inadequate for capturing what is precisely the productive aspect of power. In defining the effects of power as repression, one adopts a purely juridical conception of such power, one identifies power with a law that says no—power is taken, above all, as carrying the force of a prohibition. Now, I believe that this is a wholly negative, narrow, skeletal conception of power, one that has been curiously widespread. If power were never anything but repressive, if it never did anything but to say no, do you really think one would be brought to obey it? What makes power hold good, what makes it accepted, is simply the fact that it doesn't only weigh on us as a force that says no; it also traverses and produces things, it induces pleasure, forms knowledge, produces discourse. It needs to be considered as a productive network that runs through the whole social body, much more than as a negative instance whose function is repression. In *Discipline and Punish*, what I wanted to show was how, from the seventeenth and eighteenth centuries onward, there was a veritable technological take-off in the productivity of power. Not only did the monarchies of the Classical period develop great state apparatuses (the army, the police, and fiscal administration) but, above all, in this period what one might call a new "economy" of power was established, that is to say, procedures that allowed the effects of power to circulate in a manner at once continuous, uninterrupted, adapted, and "individualized" throughout the entire social body. These new techniques are both much more efficient and much less wasteful (less costly economically, less risky in their results, less open to loopholes and resistances) than the techniques previously employed, which were based on a mixture of more or less forced tolerances (from recognized privileges to endemic criminality) and costly ostentation (spectacular and discontinuous interventions of power, the most violent form of which was the "exemplary," because exceptional, punishment).

QUESTION: Repression is a concept used, above all, in relation to sexuality. It was held that bourgeois society represses sexuality, stifles sexual desire, and so forth. And when one considers for example the campaign launched against masturbation in the eighteenth century, or the medical discourse on homosexuality in the second half of the nineteenth century, or discourse on sexuality in general, one does seem to be faced with a discourse of repression. In reality, though, this discourse serves to make possible a whole series of interventions, tactical and positive interventions of surveillance, circulation, control, and so forth, which seem to have been intimately linked with techniques that give the appearance of repression or are at least liable to be interpreted as such. I believe the crusade against masturbation is a typical example of this.

FOUCAULT: Certainly. It is customary to say that bourgeois society repressed infantile sexuality to the point where it refused even to speak of it or acknowledge its existence. It was necessary to wait until Freud for the discovery at last to be made that children have a sexuality. Now, if you read all the books on pedagogy and child medicine—all the manuals for parents that were published in the eighteenth century—you find that children's sex is spoken of constantly and in every possible context. One might argue that the purpose of these discourses was precisely to prevent children from having a sexuality. But their *effect* was to din it into parents' heads that their children's sex constituted a fundamental problem in terms of their parental educational responsibilities, and to din it into children's heads that their relationship with their own bodies and their own sex was to be a fundamental problem as far as *they* were concerned; and this had the consequence of sexually exciting the bodies of children while at the same time fixing the parental gaze and vigilance on the peril of infantile sexuality. The result was a sexualizing of the infantile body, a sexualizing of the bodily relationship between parent and child, a sexualizing of the familial domain. "Sexuality" is far more one of the positive products of power than power was ever repressive of sex. I believe that it is precisely these positive mechanisms that need to be investigated, and here one must free oneself of the juridical schematism of all previous characterizations of the nature of power. Hence, a historical problem arises, namely that of discovering why the West has insisted for so long on seeing the power it exercises as juridical and negative rather than as technical and positive.

QUESTION: Perhaps this is because it has always been thought that power is mediated through the forms prescribed in the great juridical and philosophical theories, and that there is a fundamental, immutable gulf between those who exercise power and those who undergo it.

FOUCAULT: I wonder if this isn't bound up with the institution of monarchy. This developed during the Middle Ages against the backdrop of the previously endemic struggles between feudal power agencies. The monarchy presented itself as a referee, a power capable of putting an end to war, violence, and pillage and saying no to these struggles and private feuds. It made itself acceptable by allocating itself a juridical and negative function, albeit one whose limits it naturally began at once to overstep. Sovereign, law, and prohibition formed a system of representation of power which was extended during the subsequent era by the theories of right: political theory has never ceased to be obsessed with the person of the sovereign. Such theories still continue today to busy themselves with the problem of sovereignty. What we need, however, is a political

philosophy that isn't erected around the problem of sovereignty or, therefore, around the problems of law and prohibition. We need to cut off the king's head. In political theory that
has still to be done.

QUESTION: The king's head still hasn't been cut off, yet already
people are trying to replace it with discipline, that vast system
instituted in the seventeenth century comprising the functions
of surveillance, normalization, and control, and, a little later,
those of punishment, correction, education, and so on. One won-
ders where this system comes from, why it emerges, and what
its use is. And today there is rather a tendency to attribute a subject to it, a great, molar, totalitarian subject, namely the modern
state, constituted in the sixteenth and seventeenth centuries and
bringing with it (according to the classical theories) the professional army, the police, and the administrative bureaucracy.

FOUCAULT: To pose the problem in terms of the state means to
continue posing it in terms of sovereign and sovereignty, that is
to say, in terms of law. If one describes all these phenomena of
power as dependent on the state apparatus, this means grasp-
ing them as essentially repressive: the army as a power of
death, police and justice as punitive instances, and so on. I don't
want to say that the state isn't important; what I want to say is
that relations of power, and hence the analysis that must be
made of them, necessarily extend beyond the limits of the
state—in two senses. First of all, because the state, for all the
omnipotence of its apparatuses, is far from being able to occupy
the whole field of actual power relations; and, further, because
the state can only operate on the basis of other, already existing

power relations. The state is superstructural in relation to a whole series of power networks that invest the body, sexuality, the family, kinship, knowledge, technology, and so forth. True, these networks stand in a conditioning-conditioned relationship to a kind of "metapower" structured essentially around a certain number of great prohibition functions; but this metapower with its prohibitions can only take hold and secure its footing where it is rooted in a whole series of multiple and indefinite power relations that supply the necessary basis for the great negative forms of power. That is just what I was trying to make apparent in my book.

QUESTION: Doesn't this open up the possibility of overcoming the dualism of political struggles that eternally feed on the opposition between the state, on the one hand, and revolution, on the other? Doesn't it indicate a wider field of conflicts than that where the adversary is the state?

FOUCAULT: I would say that the state consists in the codification of a whole number of power relations that render its functioning possible, and that revolution is a different type of codification of the same relations. This implies that there are many different kinds of revolution, roughly speaking, as many kinds as there are possible subversive recodifications of power relations—and, further, that one can perfectly well conceive of revolutions that leave essentially untouched the power relations that form the basis for the functioning of the state.

QUESTION: You have said about power as an object of research that one has to invert Clausewitz's formula so as to arrive at the idea that politics is the continuation of war by other means. Does the military model seem to you on the basis of your most recent researches to be the best one for describing power; is war here simply a metaphorical model, or is it the literal, regular, everyday mode of operation of power?

FOUCAULT: This is the problem I now find myself confronting. As soon as one endeavors to detach power with its techniques and procedures from the form of law within which it has been theoretically confined up until now, one is driven to ask this basic question: Isn't power simply a form of warlike domination? Shouldn't one therefore conceive of all problems of power in terms of relations of war? Isn't power a sort of generalized war that, at particular moments, assumes the forms of peace and the state? Peace would then be a form of war, and the state a means of waging it.

A whole range of problems emerge here. Who wages war against whom? Is it between two classes, or more? Is it a war of all against all? What is the role of the army and military institutions in this civil society where permanent war is waged? What is the relevance of concepts of tactics and strategy for analyzing structures and political processes? What is the essence and mode of transformation of power relations? All these questions need to be explored. In any case, it's astonishing to see how easily and self-evidently people talk of warlike relations of power or of class struggle without ever making it clear whether some form of war is meant, and if so what form.

QUESTION: We have already talked about this disciplinary power whose effects, rules, and mode of constitution you describe in *Discipline and Punish.* One might ask here, why surveillance? What is the use of surveillance? Now, there is a phenomenon that emerges during the eighteenth century, namely the discovery of population as an object of scientific investigation; people begin to inquire into birth rates, death rates, and changes in population, and to say for the first time that it is impossible to govern a state without knowing its population. M. Moheau for example, who was one of the first to organize this kind of research on an administrative basis, seems to see its goal as lying in the problems of political control of a population. Does this disciplinary power then act alone and of itself, or rather, doesn't it draw support from something more general, namely, this fixed conception of a population that reproduces itself in the proper way, composed of people who marry in the proper way and behave in the proper way, according to precisely determined norms? One would then have, on the one hand, a sort of global, molar body, the body of the population, together with a whole series of discourses concerning it, and then, on the other hand, down below, the small bodies, the docile, individual bodies, the microbodies of discipline. Even if you are only perhaps at the beginning of your researches here, could you say how you see the nature of the relationships—if any—engendered between these different bodies: the molar body of the population and the microbodies of individuals?

FOUCAULT: Your question is exactly on target. I find it difficult to reply because I am working on this problem right now. I believe one must keep in view the fact that, along with all the fundamental technical inventions and discoveries of the seventeenth and eighteenth centuries, a new technology of the exercise of power also emerged which was probably even more important than the constitutional reforms and new forms of government established at the end of the eighteenth century. In the camp of the Left, one often hears people saying that power is that which abstracts, which negates the body, represses, suppresses, and so forth. I would say instead that what I find most striking about these new technologies of power introduced since the seventeenth and eighteenth centuries is their concrete and precise character, their grasp of a multiple and differentiated reality. In feudal societies, power functioned essentially through signs and levies. Signs of loyalty to the feudal lords, rituals, ceremonies, and so forth, and levies in the form of taxes, pillage, hunting, war, and so on. In the seventeenth and eighteenth centuries, a form of power comes into being that begins to exercise itself through social production and social service. It becomes a matter of obtaining productive service from individuals in their concrete lives. And, in consequence, a real and effective "incorporation" of power was necessary, in the sense that power had to be able to gain access to the bodies of individuals, to their acts, attitudes, and modes of everyday behavior. Hence the significance of methods such as school discipline, which succeeded in making children's bodies the object of highly complex systems of manipulation and conditioning. At the same time, though, these new techniques of power needed to grapple with the phenomena of population, in short to undertake the administration, control, and direction of the accumulation of men (the economic system that promotes the accumulation of capital and the system of power that ordains the accumulation of men are, from the seventeenth century on, correlated and inseparable phenomena): hence there arise the problems of demography, public health, hygiene,

housing conditions, longevity, and fertility. And I believe that
the political significance of the problem of sex is due to the fact
that sex is located at the point of intersection of the discipline
of the body and the control of the population.

QUESTION: Finally, a question you have been asked before: The
work you do, these preoccupations of yours, the results you arrive at, what use can one finally make of all this in everyday political struggles? You have spoken previously of local struggles
as the specific site of confrontation with power, outside and beyond all such global, general instances as parties or classes.
What does this imply about the role of intellectuals? If one isn't
an "organic" intellectual acting as the spokesman for a global
organization, if one doesn't purport to function as the bringer,
the master of truth, what position is the intellectual to assume?

FOUCAULT: For a long period, the "left" intellectual spoke, and
was acknowledged the right of speaking, in the capacity of
master of truth and justice.[1] He was heard, or purported to
make himself heard, as the spokesman of the universal. To be an
intellectual meant something like being the consciousness/
conscience of us all. I think we have here an idea transposed
from Marxism, from a faded Marxism indeed. Just as the proletariat, by the necessity of its historical situation, is the bearer
of the universal (but its immediate, unreflected bearer, barely
conscious of itself as such), so the intellectual, through his
moral, theoretical, and political choice, aspires to be the bearer
of this universality in its conscious, elaborated form. The intellectual is thus taken as the clear, individual figure of a universality whose obscure, collective form is embodied in the proletariat.

Some years have now passed since the intellectual was called upon to play this role. A new mode of the "connection between theory and practice" has been established. Intellectuals have become used to working not in the modality of the "universal," the "exemplary," the "just-and-true-for-all," but within specific sectors, at the precise points where their own conditions of life or work situate them (housing, the hospital, the asylum, the laboratory, the university, family and sexual relations). This has undoubtedly given them a much more immediate and concrete awareness of struggles. And they have met here with problems that are specific, "nonuniversal," and often different from those of the proletariat or the masses. And yet I believe intellectuals have actually been drawn closer to the proletariat and the masses, for two reasons. First, because it has been a question of real, material, everyday struggles; and second, because they have often been confronted, albeit in a different form, by the same adversary as the proletariat, namely, the multinational corporations, the judicial and police apparatuses, the property speculators, and so on. This is what I would call the "specific" intellectual as opposed to the "universal" intellectual.

This new configuration has a further political significance. It makes it possible if not to integrate them at least to rearticulate categories that were previously kept separate. The intellectual par excellence used to be the writer: as a universal consciousness, a free subject, he was counterposed to those intellectuals who were merely *competent instances* in the service of the state or capital—technicians, magistrates, teachers. Since the time when each individual's specific activity began to serve as the basis for politicization, the threshold of *writing*, as the sacralizing mark of the intellectual, has disappeared. And it has become possible to develop lateral connections across different forms of knowledge and from one focus of politicization to another. Magistrates and psychiatrists, doctors and social workers, laboratory technicians and sociologists have become able to participate—both within their own fields and through mutual exchange and support—in a global process of politicization of intellectuals. This process explains how, even as the writer tends to disappear as a figurehead, the university and the academic emerge if not as principal elements then at least as "exchangers," privileged points of intersection. If the universities and education have become politically ultrasensitive areas, this is no doubt the reason why. And what is called the "crisis of the universities" should be interpreted not as a loss of power but, on the contrary, as a multiplication and reinforcement of their power effects as centers in a polymorphous ensemble of intellectuals who virtually all pass through and relate themselves to the academic system. The whole relentless theorization of writing we saw in the sixties was doubtless only a swan song. Through it, the writer was fighting for the preservation of his political privilege. But the fact that it was precisely a matter of theory, that he needed scientific credentials (founded in linguistics, semiology, psychoanalysis), that this theory took its references from the direction of Saussure, or Chomsky, and so on, and that it gave rise to such mediocre literary products—all this proves that the activity of the writer was no longer at the focus of things.

It seems to me that this figure of the "specific" intellectual has emerged since World War II. Perhaps it was the atomic scientist (in a word or, rather, a name: Oppenheimer) who acted as the point of transition between the universal and the specific intellectual. It's because he had a direct and localized relation to scientific knowledge and institutions that the atomic scientist could make his intervention; but, since the nuclear threat affected the whole human race and the fate of the world, his discourse could at the same time be the discourse of the universal. Under the rubric of this protest, which concerned the entire world, the atomic expert brought into play his specific position in the order of knowledge. And for the first time, I think, the intellectual was hounded by political powers, no longer on account of a general discourse he conducted but because of the knowledge at his disposal: it was at this level that he constituted a political threat. I am only speaking here of Western intellectuals. What happened in the Soviet Union is analogous with this on a number of points, but different on many others. There is certainly a whole study that needs to be made of scientific dissidence in the West and the socialist countries since 1945.

It is possible to suppose that the "universal" intellectual, as he functioned in the nineteenth and early twentieth centuries, was in fact derived from a quite specific historical figure—the man of justice, the man of law, who counterposes to power, despotism, and the abuses and arrogance of wealth the universality of justice and the equity of an ideal law. The great political struggles of the eighteenth century were fought over law, right, the constitution, the just in reason and law, that which can and must apply universally. What we call today "the intellectual" (I mean the intellectual in the political not the sociological sense of the word, in other words, the person who uses his knowledge, his competence, and his relation to truth in the

field of political struggles) was, I think, an offspring of the jurist, or at any rate of the man who invoked the universality of a
just law, if necessary against the legal professions themselves
(Voltaire, in France, is the prototype of such intellectuals). The
"universal" intellectual derives from the jurist or notable, and
finds his fullest manifestation in the writer, the bearer of values
and significations in which all can recognize themselves. The
"specific" intellectual derives from quite another figure, not the
jurist or notable, but the savant or expert. I said just now that
it's with the atomic scientists that this latter figure comes to
the forefront. In fact, it was preparing in the wings for some
time before and was even present on at least a corner of the
stage from about the end of the nineteenth century. No doubt
it's with Darwin or, rather, with the post-Darwinian evolution-
ists that this figure begins to appear clearly. The stormy relationship between evolutionism and the socialists, as well as
the highly ambiguous effects of evolutionism (on sociology,
criminology, psychiatry, and eugenics, for example) mark the
important moment when the savant begins to intervene in contemporary political struggles in the name of a "local" scientific
truth—however important the latter may be. Historically, Darwin represents this point of inflection in the history of the
Western intellectual. (Zola is very significant from this point of
view: he is the type of the "universal" intellectual, bearer of law
and militant of equity, but he ballasts his discourse with a
whole invocation of nosology and evolutionism, which he believes to be scientific, though he grasps them very poorly in
any case, and whose political effects on his own discourse are
very equivocal.) If one were to study this closely, one would
have to follow how the physicists, at the turn of the century,

reentered the field of political debate. The debates between the theorists of socialism and the theorists of relativity are of capital importance in this history.

At all events, biology and physics were to a privileged degree the zones of formation of this new personage, the specific intellectual. The extension of technico-scientific structures in the economic and strategic domain was what gave him his real importance. The figure in which the functions and prestige of this new intellectual are concentrated is no longer that of the "writer of genius" but that of the "absolute savant," no longer he who bears the values of all, opposes the unjust sovereign or his ministers, and makes his cry resound even beyond the grave. It is, rather, he who, along with a handful of others, has at his disposal—whether in the service of the state or against it—powers that can either benefit or irrevocably destroy life. He is no longer the rhapsodist of the eternal but the strategist of life and death. Meanwhile, we are at present experiencing the disappearance of the figure of the "great writer."

Now let's come back to more precise details. We accept, alongside the development of technico-scientific structures in contemporary society, the importance gained by the specific intellectual in recent decades, as well as the acceleration of this process since around 1960. Now, the "specific" intellectual encounters certain obstacles and faces certain dangers. The danger of remaining at the level of conjunctural struggles, pressing demands restricted to particular sectors. The risk of letting himself be manipulated by the political parties or trade union apparatuses that control these local struggles. Above all, the risk of being unable to develop these struggles for lack of a global strategy or outside support—the risk, too, of not being followed, or only by very limited groups. In France, we can see at the moment an example of this. The struggle around the prisons, the penal system, and the police-judicial system, because it has developed "in solitary," among social workers and ex-prisoners, has tended increasingly to separate itself from the forces that would have enabled it to grow. It has allowed itself to be penetrated by a whole naive, archaic ideology that makes the criminal at once into the innocent victim and the pure rebel—society's scapegoat—and the young wolf of future revolutions. This return to anarchist themes of the late nineteenth century was possible only because of a failure of integration of current strategies. And the result has been a deep split between this campaign with its monotonous, lyrical little chant, heard only among a few small groups, and the masses who have good reason not to accept it as valid political currency, but who also—thanks to the studiously cultivated fear of criminals—tolerate the maintenance or, rather, the reinforcement of the judicial and police apparatuses.

It seems to me that we are now at a point where the function of the specific intellectual needs to be reconsidered. Reconsidered but not abandoned, despite the nostalgia of some for the great "universal" intellectuals and the desire for a new philosophy, a new worldview. Suffice it to consider the important results that have been achieved in psychiatry: they prove that these local, specific struggles haven't been a mistake and haven't led to a dead end. One may even say that the role of the specific intellectual must become more and more important in proportion to the political responsibilities which he is obliged willy-nilly to accept, as a nuclear scientist, computer expert, pharmacologist, and so on. It would be a dangerous error to discount him politically in his specific relation to a local form of power, either on the grounds that this is a specialist matter that doesn't concern the masses (which is doubly wrong: they are already aware of it, and in any case implicated in it), or that the specific intellectual serves the interests of state or capital (which is true, but at the same time shows the strategic position he occupies); or again, on the grounds that he propagates a scientific ideology (which isn't always true, and is anyway certainly a secondary matter compared with the fundamental point: the effects proper to true discourses).

The important thing here, I believe, is that truth isn't outside power or lacking in power: contrary to a myth whose history and functions would repay further study, truth isn't the reward of free spirits, the child of protracted solitude, nor the privilege of those who have succeeded in liberating themselves. Truth is a thing of this world: it is produced only by virtue of multiple forms of constraint. And it induces regular effects of power. Each society has its regime of truth, its "general politics" of truth—that is, the types of discourse it accepts and makes function as true; the mechanisms and instances that enable one to distinguish true and false statements; the means by which each is sanctioned; the techniques and procedures accorded value in the acquisition of truth; the status of those who are charged with saying what counts as true.

In societies like ours, the "political economy" of truth is characterized by five important traits. "Truth" is centered on the form of scientific discourse and the institutions that produce it; it is subject to constant economic and political incitement (the demand for truth, as much for economic production as for political power); it is the object, under diverse forms, of immense diffusion and consumption (circulating through apparatuses of education and information whose extent is relatively broad in the social body, notwithstanding certain strict limitations); it is produced and transmitted under the control, dominant if not exclusive, of a few great political and economic apparatuses (university, army, writing, media); finally, it is the issue of a whole political debate and social confrontation ("ideological" struggles).

It seems to me that what must now be taken into account in the intellectual is not the "bearer of universal values." Rather, it's the person occupying a specific position—but whose specificity is linked, in a society like ours, to the general functioning of an apparatus of truth. In other words, the intellectual has a threefold specificity: that of his class position (whether as petit bourgeois in the service of capitalism or "organic" intellectual of the proletariat); that of his conditions of life and work, linked to his condition as an intellectual (his field of research, his place in a laboratory, the political and economic demands to which he submits or against which he rebels, in the university, the hospital, and so on); finally, the specificity of the politics of truth in our societies. And it's with this last factor that his position can take on a general significance, and that his local, specific struggle can have effects and implications that are not simply professional or sectoral. The intellectual can operate and struggle at the general level of that regime of truth so essential to the structure and functioning of our society. There is a battle "for truth," or at least "around truth"—it being understood once again that by truth I mean not "the ensemble of truths to be discovered and accepted" but, rather, "the ensemble of rules according to which the true and the false are separated and specific effects of power attached to the true," it being understood also that it's not a matter of a battle "on behalf" of the truth but of a battle about the status of truth and the economic and political role it plays. It is necessary to think of the political problems of intellectuals not in terms of "science" and "ideology" but in terms of "truth" and "power." And thus the question of the professionalization of intellectuals and the division between intellectual and manual labor can be envisaged in a new way.

All this must seem very confused and uncertain. Uncertain indeed, and what I am saying here is, above all, to be taken as a hypothesis. In order for it to be a little less confused, however, I would like to put forward a few "propositions"—not firm assertions but simply suggestions to be further tested and evaluated.

"Truth" is to be understood as a system of ordered procedures for the production, regulation, distribution, circulation, and operation of statements.

"Truth" is linked in a circular relation with systems of power that produce and sustain it, and to effects of power which it induces and which extend it—a "regime" of truth.

This regime is not merely ideological or superstructural; it was a condition of the formation and development of capitalism. And it's this same regime which, subject to certain modifications, operates in the socialist countries (I leave open here the question of China, about which I know little).

The essential political problem for the intellectual is not to criticize the ideological contents supposedly linked to science, or to ensure that his own scientific practice is accompanied by a correct ideology, but that of ascertaining the possibility of constituting a new politics of truth. The problem is not changing people's consciousnesses—or what's in their heads—but the political, economic, institutional regime of the production of truth.

It's not a matter of emancipating truth from every system of power (which would be a chimera, for truth is already power) but of detaching the power of truth from the forms of hegemony, social, economic, and cultural, within which it operates at the present time.

The political question, to sum up, is not error, illusion, alienated consciousness, or ideology; it is truth itself. Hence the importance of Nietzsche.

Notes

1. Foucault's response to this final question was given in writing.

5.

"Omnes et Singulatim": Toward a Critique of Political Reason

Michel Foucault

I

The title sounds pretentious, I know. But the reason for that is precisely its own excuse. Since the nineteenth century, Western thought has never stopped laboring at the task of criticizing the role of reason—or the lack of reason—in political structures. It's therefore perfectly unfitting to undertake such a vast project once again. However, so many previous attempts are a warrant that every new venture will be just about as successful as the former ones—and in any case, probably just as fortunate.

Under such a banner, mine is the embarrassment of one who has only sketches and incompletable drafts to propose. Philosophy gave up trying to offset the impotence of scientific reason long ago; it no longer tries to complete its edifice.

One of the Enlightenment's tasks was to multiply reason's political powers. But the men of the nineteenth century soon started wondering whether reason wasn't getting too powerful in our societies. They began to worry about a relationship they confusedly suspected between a rationalization-prone society and certain threats to the individual and his liberties, to the species and its survival.

In other words, since Kant, the role of philosophy has been to prevent reason from going beyond the limits of what is given in experience; but from the same moment—that is, from the development of modern states and political management of society—the role of philosophy has also been to keep watch over the excessive powers of political rationality, which is rather a promising life expectancy.

Everybody is aware of such banal facts. But that they are banal does not mean they don't exist. What we have to do with banal facts is to discover, to try to discover, which specific and perhaps original problems are connected with them.

The relationship between rationalization and the excesses of political power is evident. And we should not need to wait for bureaucracy or concentration camps to recognize the existence of such relations. But the problem is what to do with such an evident fact.

Shall we "try" reason? To my mind, nothing would be more sterile. First, because the field has nothing to do with guilt or innocence. Second, because it's senseless to refer to "reason" as the contrary entity to nonreason. Last, because such a trial would trap us into playing the arbitrary and boring part of either the rationalist or the irrationalist.

Shall we investigate this kind of rationalism that seems to be specific to our modern culture and originates in Enlightenment? I think that that was the way of some of the members of the Frankfurt school. My purpose is not to begin a discussion of their works—they are most important and valuable. I would suggest another way of investigating the links between rationalization and power:

1. It may be wise not to take as a whole the rationalization of society or of culture, but to analyze this process in several fields, each of them grounded in a fundamental experience: madness, illness, death, crime, sexuality, and so on.

2. I think that the word *rationalization* is a dangerous one. The main problem when people try to rationalize something is not to investigate whether or not they conform to principles of rationality but to discover which kind of rationality they are using.

3. Even if the Enlightenment has been a very important phase in our history, and in the development of political technology, I think we have to refer to much more remote processes if we want to understand how we have been trapped in our own history.

This was my modus operandi in my previous work—to analyze the relations between experiences like madness, death, crime, sexuality, and several technologies of power. What I am working on now is the problem of individuality—or, I should say, self-identity in relation to the problem of "individualizing power."

Everyone knows that in European societies political power has evolved toward more and more centralized forms. Historians have been studying this organization of the state, with its administration and bureaucracy, for dozens of years.

I'd like to suggest in these two lectures the possibility of analyzing another kind of transformation in such power relationships. This transformation is, perhaps, less celebrated. But I think that it is also important, mainly for modern societies. Apparently, this evolution seems antagonistic to the evolution toward a centralized state. What I mean in fact is the development of power techniques oriented toward individuals and intended to rule them in a continuous and permanent way. If the state is the political form of a centralized and centralizing power, let us call pastorship the individualizing power.

My purpose this evening is to outline the origin of this pastoral modality of power, or at least some aspects of its ancient history. And in the next lecture, I'll try to show how this pastorship happened to combine with its opposite, the state.

The idea of the deity, or the king, or the leader, as a shepherd followed by a flock of sheep wasn't familiar to the Greeks and Romans. There were exceptions, I know—early ones in Homeric literature, later ones in certain texts of the Lower Empire. I'll come back to them later. Roughly speaking, we can say that the metaphor of the flock didn't occur in great Greek or Roman political literature.

This is not the case in ancient Oriental societies—Egypt, Assyria, Judaea. Pharaoh was an Egyptian shepherd. Indeed, he ritually received the herdsman's crook on his coronation day; and the term "shepherd of men" was one of the Babylonian monarch's titles. But God was also a shepherd leading men to their grazing ground and ensuring them food. An Egyptian hymn invoked Ra this way: "O Ra that keepest watch when all men sleep, Thou who seekest what is good for thy cattle . . ." The association between God and king is easily made, since both assume the same role: the flock they watch over is the same; the shepherd-king is entrusted with the great divine shepherd's creatures. An Assyrian invocation to the king ran like this: "Illustrious companion of pastures, Thou who carest for thy land and feedest it, shepherd of all abundance."

But, as we know, it was the Hebrews who developed and intensified the pastoral theme—with nevertheless a highly peculiar characteristic: God, and God only, is his people's shepherd. With just one positive exception: David, as the founder of the monarchy, is the only one to be referred to as a shepherd. God gave him the task of assembling a flock.

There are negative exceptions, too. Wicked kings are consistently compared to bad shepherds; they disperse the flock, let it die of thirst, shear it solely for profit's sake. Yahweh is the one and only true shepherd. He guides his own people in person, aided only by his prophets. As the Psalms say: "Like a flock / hast Thou led Thy people, by Moses's and by Aaron's hand." Of course, I can treat neither the historical problems pertaining to the origin of this comparison nor its evolution throughout Jewish thought. I just want to show a few themes typical of pastoral power. I'd like to point out the contrast with Greek political thought, and to show how important these themes became in Christian thought and institutions later on.

1. The shepherd wields power over a flock rather than over a land. It's probably much more complex than that, but, broadly speaking, the relation between the deity,

the land, and men differs from that of the Greeks. Their gods owned the land, and this primary possession determined the relationship between men and gods. On the contrary, it's the Shepherd-God's relationship with his flock that is primary and fundamental here. God gives, or promises, his flock a land.

2. The shepherd gathers together, guides, and leads his flock. The idea that the political leader was to quiet any hostilities within the city and make unity reign over conflict is undoubtedly present in Greek thought. But what the shepherd gathers together is dispersed individuals. They gather together on hearing his voice: "I'll whistle and will gather them together." Conversely, the shepherd only has to disappear for the flock to be scattered. In other words, the shepherd's immediate presence and direct action cause the flock to exist. Once the good Greek lawgiver, like Solon, has resolved any conflicts, what he leaves behind him is a strong city with laws enabling it to endure without him.

3. The shepherd's role is to ensure the salvation of his flock. The Greeks said also that the deity saved the city; they never stopped declaring that the competent leader is a helmsman warding his ship away from the rocks. But the way the shepherd saves his flock is quite different. It's not only a matter of saving them all, all together, when danger comes nigh. It's a matter of constant, individualized, and final kindness. Constant kindness, for the shepherd ensures his flock's food; every day he attends to their thirst and hunger. The Greek god was asked to provide a fruitful land and

abundant crops. He wasn't asked to foster a flock day by
day. And individualized kindness, too, for the shepherd
sees that all the sheep, each and every one of them, is fed
and saved. Later Hebrew literature, especially, laid the
emphasis on such individually kindly power: a rabbinical commentary on Exodus explains why Yahweh chose
Moses to shepherd his people: he had left his flock to go
and search for one lost sheep.

Last and not least, it's final kindness. The shepherd
has a target for his flock. It must either be led to good
grazing ground or brought back to the fold.

4. Yet another difference lies in the idea that wielding
power is a "duty." The Greek leader, naturally, had to
make decisions in the interest of all; he would have been
a bad leader had he preferred his personal interest. But
his duty was a glorious one: even if in war he had to give
up his life, such a sacrifice was offset by something extremely precious—immortality. He never lost. By way
of contrast, shepherdly kindness is much closer to "devotedness." Everything the shepherd does is geared to
the good of his flock. That's his constant concern.
When they sleep, *he* keeps watch.

The theme of keeping watch is important. It brings
out two aspects of the shepherd's devotedness. First, he
acts, he works, he puts himself out, for those he nour-
ishes and who are asleep. Second, he watches over them.
He pays attention to them all and scans each one of
them. He's got to know his flock as a whole, and in detail. Not only must he know where good pastures are,

the seasons' laws, and the order of things; he must also know each one's particular needs. Once again, a rabbinical commentary on Exodus describes Moses's qualities as a shepherd in this way: he would send each sheep in turn to graze—first, the youngest, for them to browse on the tenderest sward; then the older ones; and last the oldest, who were capable of browsing on the roughest grass. The shepherd's power implies individual attention paid to each member of the flock.

These are just themes that Hebraic texts associate with the metaphors of the Shepherd-God and his flock of people. In no way do I claim that that is effectively how political power was wielded in Hebrew society before the fall of Jerusalem. I do not even claim that such a conception of political power is in any way coherent.

They're just themes. Paradoxical, even contradictory, ones. Christianity was to give them considerable importance, both in the Middle Ages and in modern times. Among all the societies in history, ours—I mean, those that came into being at the end of Antiquity on the Western side of the European continent— have perhaps been the most aggressive and the most conquering; they have been capable of the most stupefying violence, against themselves as well as against others. They invented a great many different political forms. They profoundly altered their legal structures several times. It must be kept in mind that they alone evolved a strange technology of power treating the vast majority of men as a flock with a few as shepherds. Thus, they established between them a series of complex, continuous, and paradoxical relationships.

This is undoubtedly something singular in the course of history. Clearly, the development of "pastoral technology" in the management of men profoundly disrupted the structures of ancient society.

So as to better explain the importance of this disruption, I'd like to briefly return to what I was saying about the Greeks. I can see the objections liable to be made.

One is that the Homeric poems use the shepherd metaphor to refer to the kings. In the *Iliad* and the *Odyssey*, the expression *poimēn laon* crops up several times. It qualifies the leaders, highlighting the grandeur of their power. Moreover, it's a ritual title, common in even late Indo-European literature. In *Beowulf*, the king is still regarded as a shepherd. But there is nothing really surprising in the fact that the same title, as in the Assyrian texts, is to be found in archaic epic poems.

The problem arises, rather, as to Greek thought: there is at least one category of texts where references to shepherd models are made—the Pythagorean ones. The metaphor of the herdsman appears in the *Fragments* of Archytas, quoted by Stobeus. The word *nomos* (the law) is connected with the word *nomeus* (shepherd): the shepherd shares out, the law apportions. Then Zeus is called Nomios and Nemeios because he gives his sheep food. And, finally, the magistrate must be *philanthrōpos*, that is, devoid of selfishness. He must be full of zeal and solicitude, like a shepherd.

B. Grube, the German editor of Archytas's *Fragments*, says that this proves a Hebrew influence unique in Greek literature. Other commentators, such as Armand Delatte, say that the comparison between gods, magistrates, and shepherds was common in Greece; it is therefore not to be dwelt upon.

I shall restrict myself to political literature. The results of the inquiry are clear: the political metaphor of the shepherd occurs neither in Isocrates, nor in Demosthenes, nor in Aristotle. This is rather surprising when one reflects that in his *Areopagiticus*, Isocrates insists on the magistrates' duties; he stresses the need for them to be devoted and to show concern for young people. Yet not a word as to any shepherd.

By contrast, Plato often speaks of the shepherd-magistrate. He mentions the idea in *Critias, The Republic*, and *Laws*. He thrashes it out in *The Statesman*. In the former, the shepherd theme is rather subordinate. Sometimes, those happy days when mankind was governed directly by the gods and grazed on abundant pastures are evoked (*Critias*). Sometimes, the magistrates' necessary virtue—as contrasted with Thrasymachos's vice, is what is insisted upon (*The Republic*). And sometimes, the problem is to define the subordinate magistrates' role: indeed, they, just as the watchdogs, have to obey "those at the top of the scale" (*Laws*).

But in *The Statesman*, pastoral power is the central problem, and it is treated at length. Can the city's decision-maker, can the commander, be defined as a sort of shepherd?

Plato's analysis is well known. To solve this question he uses the division method. A distinction is drawn between the man who conveys orders to inanimate things (for example, the architect) and the man who gives orders to animals; between the man who gives orders to isolated animals (like a yoke of oxen) and he who gives orders to flocks; and he who gives orders to animal flocks, and he who commands human flocks. And there we have the political leader—a shepherd of men.

But this first division remains unsatisfactory. It has to be pushed further. The method of opposing *men* to all the other animals isn't a good one. And so the dialogue starts all over again. A whole series of distinctions is established: between wild animals and tame ones; those which live in water and those which live on land; those with horns and those without; between cleft- and plain-hoofed animals; between those capable and incapable of mutual reproduction. And the dialogue wanders astray with these never-ending subdivisions.

So, what do the initial development of the dialogue and its subsequent failure show? That the division method can prove nothing at all when it isn't managed correctly. It also shows that the idea of analyzing political power as the relationship between a shepherd and his animals was probably a rather controversial one at the time. Indeed, it's the first assumption to cross the interlocutors' minds when seeking to discover the essence of the politician. Was it a commonplace at the time? Or, rather, was Plato discussing one of the Pythagorean themes? The absence of the shepherd metaphor in other contemporary political texts seems to tip the scale toward the second hypothesis. But we can probably leave the discussion open.

My personal inquiry bears upon how Plato impugns the theme in the rest of the dialogue. He does so first by means of methodological arguments, then by means of the celebrated myth of the world revolving around its spindle.

The methodological arguments are extremely interesting. Whether the king is a sort of shepherd or not can be told not by deciding which different species can form a flock but, rather, by analyzing what the shepherd does.

What is characteristic of his task? First, the shepherd is alone at the head of his flock. Second, his job is to supply his cattle with food; to care for them when they are sick; to play

them music to get them together, and guide them; to arrange
their intercourse with a view to the finest offspring. So we *do*
find the typical shepherd metaphor themes of Oriental texts.

And what's the king's task in regard to all this? Like the
shepherd, he is alone at the head of the city. But, for the rest,
who provides mankind with food? The king? No. The farmer,
the baker do. Who looks after men when they are sick? The
king? No. The physician. And who guides them with music?
The gymnasiarch—not the king. And so, many citizens could
quite legitimately claim the title "shepherd of men." Just as the
human flock's shepherd has many rivals, so has the politician.
Consequently, if we want to find out what the politician really
and essentially is, we must sift it out from "the surrounding
flood," thereby demonstrating in what ways he *isn't* a shepherd.

Plato therefore resorts to the myth of the world revolving
around its axis in two successive and contrary motions.

In a first phase, each animal species belonged to a flock led
by a genius-shepherd. The human flock was led by the deity itself. It could lavishly avail itself of the fruits of the earth; it
needed no abode; and, after death, men came back to life. A crucial sentence adds: "The deity being their shepherd, mankind
needed no political constitution."

In a second phase, the world turned in the opposite direction. The gods were no longer men's shepherds; men had to
look after themselves, for they had been given fire. What would
the politician's role then be? Would *he* become the shepherd in
the gods' stead? Not at all. His job was to weave a strong fabric
for the city. Being a politician didn't mean feeding, nursing,
and breeding offspring but, rather, binding: binding different
virtues; binding contrary temperaments (either impetuous or

moderate), using the "shuttle" of popular opinion. The royal art of ruling consisted in gathering lives together "into a community based upon concord and friendship," and so he wove "the finest of fabrics." The entire population, "slaves and free men alike, were mantled in its folds."

The Statesman therefore seems to be classical Antiquity's most systematic reflection on the theme of the pastorate that was later to become so important in the Christian West. That we are discussing it seems to prove that a perhaps initially Oriental theme was important enough in Plato's day to deserve investigation, but I stress the fact that it was impugned.

Not impugned entirely, however. Plato did admit that the physician, the farmer, the gymnasiarch, and the pedagogue acted as shepherds. But he refused to get them involved with the politician's activity. He said so explicitly: How would the politician ever find the time to come and sit by each person, feed him, give him concerts, and care for him when sick? Only a god in a golden age could ever act like that; or again, like a physician or pedagogue, be responsible for the lives and development of a few individuals. But, situated between the two— the gods and the swains—the men who hold political power are not to be shepherds. Their task doesn't consist in fostering the life of a group of individuals. It consists in forming and assuring the city's unity. In short, the political problem is that of the relation between the one and the many in the framework of the city and its citizens. The pastoral problem concerns the lives of individuals.

All this seems very remote, perhaps. The reason for my insisting on these ancient texts is that they show us how early this problem—or rather, this series of problems—arose. They span the entirely of Western history. They are still quite important for contemporary society. They deal with the relations between political power at work within the state as a legal framework of unity, and a power we can call "pastoral," whose role is to constantly ensure, sustain, and improve the lives of each and every one.

The well-known "welfare state problem" does not only bring the needs or the new governmental techniques of today's world to light. It must be recognized for what it is: one of the extremely numerous reappearances of the tricky adjustment between political power wielded over legal subjects and pastoral power wielded over live individuals.

Obviously, I have no intention whatsoever of recounting the evolution of pastoral power throughout Christianity. The immense problems this would raise can easily be imagined: from doctrinal problems, such as Christ's denomination as "the good shepherd," right up to institutional ones such as parochial organization or the way pastoral responsibilities were shared between priests and bishops.

All I want to do is bring to light two or three aspects I regard as important for the evolution of pastorship, that is, the technology of power.

First of all, let us examine the theoretical elaboration of the theme in ancient Christian literature: Chyrsostom, Cyprian, Ambrose, Jerome, and, for monastic life, Cassian or Benedict. The Hebrew themes are considerably altered in at least four ways:

1. First, with regard to responsibility. We saw that the shepherd was to assume responsibility for the destiny of the whole flock and of each and every sheep. In the

Christian conception, the shepherd must render an account—not only of each sheep, but of all their actions, all the good or evil they are liable to do, all that happens to them.

Moreover, between each sheep and its shepherd Christianity conceives a complex exchange and circulation of sins and merits. The sheep's sin is also imputable to the shepherd. He'll have to render an account of it at the Final Judgment. Conversely, by helping his flock to find salvation, the shepherd will also find his own. But by saving his sheep, he lays himself open to getting lost; so if he wants to save himself, he must run the risk of losing himself for others. If he does get lost, it is the flock that will incur the greatest danger. But let's leave all these paradoxes aside. My aim was just to underline the force and complexity of the moral ties binding the shepherd to each member of his flock. And what I especially wanted to underline was that such ties not only concerned individuals' lives but the details of their actions as well.

2. The second important alteration concerns the problem of obedience. In the Hebrew conception, God being a shepherd, the flock following him complies to his will, to his law.

Christianity, on the other hand, conceived the shepherd-sheep relationship as one of individual and complete dependence. This is undoubtedly one of the points at which Christian pastorship radically diverged from Greek thought. If a Greek had to obey, he did so because it was the law, or the will of the city. If he did happen to follow the will of someone in particular (a physician, an orator, a pedagogue), then that person had rationally persuaded him to do so. And it had to be for a strictly determined aim: to be cured, to acquire a skill, to make the best choice.

In Christianity, the tie with the shepherd is an individual one. It is personal submission to him. His will is done, not because it is consistent with the law, and not just as far as it is consistent with it, but, principally, because it is his *will*. In Cassian's *Cenobitical Institutions*, there are many edifying anecdotes in which the monk finds salvation by carrying out the absurdest of his superior's orders. Obedience is a virtue. This means that it is not, as for the Greeks, a provisional means to an end but, rather, an end in itself. It is a permanent state; the sheep must permanently submit to their pastors— *subditi*. As Saint Benedict says, monks do not live according to their own free will; their wish is to be under the abbot's command—*ambulantes alieno judicio et imperio*. Greek Christianity named this state of obedience *apatheia*. The evolution of the word's meaning is significant. In Greek philosophy, apatheia denotes the control that the individual, thanks to the exercise of reason, can exert over his passions. In Christian thought, pathos is willpower exerted over oneself, for oneself. Apatheia delivers us from such willfulness.

3. Christian pastorship implies a peculiar type of knowledge between the pastor and each of his sheep.

This knowledge is particular. It individualizes. It isn't enough to know the state of the flock. That of each sheep must also be known. The theme existed long before there was Christian pastorship, but it was considerably amplified in three different ways. The shepherd must be informed as to the material needs of each member of the flock and provide for them when necessary. He must know what is going on, what each of them does—his public sins. Last but not least, he must know what goes on in the soul of each one, that is, his secret sins, his progress on the road to sanctity.

In order to ensure this individual knowledge, Christianity appropriated two essential instruments at work in the Hellenistic world—self-examination and the guidance of conscience. It took them over, but not without altering them considerably.

It is well known that self-examination was widespread among the Pythagoreans, the Stoics, and the Epicureans as a means of daily taking stock of the good or evil performed in regard to one's duties. One's progress on the way to perfection (that is, self-mastery) and the domination of one's passions could thus be measured. The guidance of conscience was also predominant in certain cultured circles, but as advice given—and sometimes paid for—in particularly difficult circumstances: in mourning, or when one was suffering a setback.

Christian pastorship closely associated these two practices. On one hand, conscience-guiding constituted a constant bind: the sheep didn't let itself be led only to come through any rough passage victoriously, it let itself be led every second. Being guided was a state, and you were fatally lost if you tried to escape it. The ever-quoted phrase runs like this: He who suffers not guidance withers away like a dead leaf. As for self-examination, its aim was not to close self-awareness in upon itself but, rather, to enable it to open up entirely to its director—to unveil to him the depths of the soul.

There are a great many first-century ascetic and monastic texts concerning the link between guidance and self-examination which show how crucial these techniques were for Christianity and how complex they had already become. What I would like to emphasize is that they delineate the emergence of a very strange phenomenon in Greco-Roman civilization, that is, the organization of a link between total obedience, knowledge of oneself, and confession to someone else.

4. There is another transformation—maybe the most important. All those Christian techniques of examination, confession, guidance, obedience, have an aim: to get individuals to work at their own "mortification" in this world. Mortification is not death, of course, but it is a renunciation of this world and of oneself, a kind of everyday death—a death that is supposed to provide life in another world. This is not the first time we see the shepherd theme associated with death; but here it is different than in the Greek idea of political power. It is not a sacrifice for the city: Christian mortification is a kind of relation of oneself to oneself. It is a part, a constitutive part of Christian self-identity.

We can say that Christian pastorship has introduced a
game that neither the Greeks nor the Hebrews imagined. It is a
strange game whose elements are life, death, truth, obedience,
individuals, self-identity—a game that seems to have nothing
to do with the game of the city surviving through the sacrifice
of the citizens. Our societies proved to be really demonic since
they happened to combine those two games—the city-citizen
game and the shepherd-flock game—in what we call the modern states.

As you may notice, what I have been trying to do this
evening is not to solve a problem but to suggest a way to approach a problem. This problem is similar to those I have been
working on since my first book about insanity and mental illness. As I told you previously, this problem deals with the relations between experiences (like madness, illness, transgression
of laws, sexuality, self-identity), knowledge (like psychiatry,
medicine, criminology, sexology, psychology), and power (such
as the power wielded in psychiatric and penal institutions, and
in all other institutions that deal with individual control).

Our civilization has developed the most complex system of
knowledge, the most sophisticated structures of power. What
has this kind of knowledge, this type of power made of us? In
what way are those fundamental experiences of madness, suffering, death, crime, desire, individuality connected—even if
we are not aware of it—with knowledge and power? I am sure
I'll never get the answer; but that does not mean that we don't
have to ask the question.

II

I have tried to show how primitive Christianity shaped the idea of a pastoral influence continuously exerting itself on individuals and through the demonstration of their particular truth. And I have tried to show how this idea of pastoral power was foreign to Greek thought despite a certain number of borrowings such as practical self-examination and the guidance of conscience.

I would like at this time, leaping across many centuries, to describe another episode that has been in itself particularly important in the history of this government of individuals by their own verity.

This instance concerns the formation of the state in the modern sense of the word. If I make this historical connection, it is obviously not in order to suggest that the aspect of pastoral power disappeared during the ten great centuries of Christian Europe, Catholic and Roman, but it seems to me that this period, contrary to what one might expect, has not been that of the triumphant pastorate. And that is true for several reasons: some are of an economic nature—the pastorate of souls is an especially urban experience, difficult to reconcile with the poor and extensive rural economy at the beginning of the Middle Ages. The other reasons are of a cultural nature: the pastorate is a complicated technique that demands a certain level of culture, not only on the part of the pastor but also among his flock. Other reasons relate to the sociopolitical structure. Feudality developed between individuals a tissue of personal bonds of an altogether different type than the pastorate.

I do not wish to say that the idea of a pastoral government

of men disappeared entirely in the medieval church. It has, indeed, remained and one can even say that it has shown great vitality. Two series of facts tend to prove this. First, the reforms that had been made in the church itself, especially in the monastic orders—the different reforms operating successively inside existing monasteries—had the goal of restoring the rigor of pastoral order among the monks themselves. As for the newly created orders—Dominican and Franciscan—essentially they proposed to perform pastoral work among the faithful. The church tried ceaselessly during successive crises to regain its pastoral functions. But there is more. In the population itself one sees all during the Middle Ages the development of a long series of struggles whose object was pastoral power. Critics of the church that fails in its obligations reject its hierarchical structure, look for the more or less spontaneous forms of community in which the flock could find the shepherd it needed. This search for pastoral expression took on numerous aspects, at times extremely violent struggles, as was the case for the Vaudois, sometimes peaceful quests as among the Frères de la Vie community. Sometimes it stirred very extensive movements such as the Hussites, sometimes it fermented limited groups like the Amis de Dieu de l'Oberland. Some of these movements were close to heresy, as among the Beghards; others were at times stirring orthodox movements that dwelled within the bosom of the church (like that of the Italian Oratorians in the fifteenth century).

I raise all of this in a very allusive manner in order to emphasize that if the pastorate was not instituted as an effective, practical government of men during the Middle Ages, it has been a permanent concern and a stake in constant struggles.

There was, across the entire period of the Middle Ages, a yearning to arrange pastoral relations among men, and this aspiration affected both the mystical tide and the great millenarian dreams.

Of course, I don't intend to treat here the problem of how states are formed. Nor do I intend to go into the different economic, social, and political processes from which they stem. Neither do I want to analyze the different institutions or mechanisms with which states equipped themselves in order to ensure their survival. I'd just like to give some fragmentary indications as to something midway between the state as a type of political organization and its mechanisms, namely, the type of rationality implemented in the exercise of state power.

I mentioned this in my first lecture. Rather than wonder whether aberrant state power is due to excessive rationalism or irrationalism, I think it would be more appropriate to pin down the specific type of political rationality the state produced.

After all, at least in this respect, political practices resemble scientific ones: it's not "reason in general" that is implemented but always a very specific type of rationality.

The striking thing is that the rationality of state power was reflective and perfectly aware of its specificity. It was not tucked away in spontaneous, blind practices. It was not brought to light by some retrospective analysis. It was formulated especially in two sets of doctrine: the *reason of state* and the *theory of police*. These two phrases soon acquired narrow and pejorative meanings, I know. But for the 150 or 200 years during which modern states were formed, their meaning was much broader than now.

The doctrine of reason of state attempted to define how the principles and methods of state government differed, say, from the way God governed the world, the father his family, or a superior his community.

The doctrine of the police defines the nature of the objects of the state's rational activity; it defines the nature of the aims it pursues, the general form of the instruments involved.

So, what I'd like to speak about today is the system of rationality. But first, there are two preliminaries: First, Friedrich Meinecke having published a most important book on reason of state, I'll speak mainly of the policing theory. Second, Germany and Italy underwent the greatest difficulties in getting established as states, and they produced the greatest number of reflections on reason of state and the police. I'll often refer to the Italian and German texts.

Let's begin with *reason of state*. Here are a few definitions:

Botero: "A perfect knowledge of the means through which states form, strengthen themselves, endure, and grow."

Palazzo (*Discourse on Government and True Reason of State*, 1606): "A rule or art enabling us to discover how to establish peace and order within the Republic."

Chemnitz (*De Ratione status*, 1647): "A certain political consideration required for all public matters, councils, and projects, whose only aim is the state's preservation, expansion, and felicity; to which end, the easiest and promptest means are to be employed."

Let me consider certain features these definitions have in common.

1. Reason of state is regarded as an "art," that is, a technique conforming to certain rules. These rules do not simply pertain to customs or traditions, but to knowledge—rational knowledge. Nowadays, the expression "reason of state" evokes "arbitrariness" or "violence." But at the time, what people had in mind was a rationality specific to the art of governing states.

2. From where does this specific art of government draw its rationale? The answer to this question provokes the scandal of nascent political thought. And yet it's very simple: the art of governing is rational, if reflection causes it to observe the nature of what is governed—here, the *state*.

   Now, to state such a platitude is to break with a simultaneously Christian and judiciary tradition, a tradition that claimed that government was essentially just. It respected a whole system of laws: human laws, the law of nature, divine law.

   There is a quite significant text by Aquinas on these points. He recalls that "art, in its field, must imitate what nature carries out in its own"; it is only reasonable under that condition. The king's government of his kingdom must imitate God's government of nature or, again, the soul's government of the body. The king must found cities just as God created the world, just as the soul gives form to the body. The king must also lead men toward their finality, just as God does for natural beings, or as the soul does when directing the body. And what is man's finality? What's good for the body? No;

he'd need only a physician, not a king. Wealth? No; a
steward would suffice. Truth? Not even that, for only a
teacher would be needed. Man needs someone capable
of opening up the way to heavenly bliss through his
conformity, here on earth, to what is *honestum*.

As we can see, the model for the art of government
is that of God imposing his laws upon his creatures.
Aquinas's model for rational government is not a political one, whereas what the sixteenth and seventeenth
centuries seek under the denomination "reason of state"
are principles capable of guiding an actual government. They aren't concerned with nature and its laws
in general—they're concerned with what the state is;
what its exigencies are.

And so we can understand the religious scandal
aroused by such a type of research. It explains why reason of state was assimilated to atheism. In France, in
particular, the expression generated in a political context was commonly associated with "atheist."

3. Reason of state is also opposed to another tradition. In
The Prince, Machiavelli's problem is to decide how a
province or territory acquired through inheritance or
by conquest can be held against its internal or external
rivals. Machiavelli's entire analysis is aimed at defining
what keeps up or reinforces the link between prince and
state, whereas the problem posed by reason of state is
that of the very existence and nature of the state itself.
This is why the theoreticians of reason of state tried to
stay aloof from Machiavelli; he had a bad reputation,

and they couldn't recognize their own problem in his. Conversely, those opposed to reason of state tried to impair this new art of governing, denouncing it as Machiavelli's legacy. However, despite these confused quarrels a century after *The Prince* had been written, *reason of state* marks the emergence of an extremely—albeit only partly—different type of rationality from Machiavelli's.

The aim of such an art of governing is precisely not to reinforce the power a prince can wield over his domain: its aim is to reinforce the state itself. This is one of the most characteristic features of all the definitions that the sixteenth and seventeenth centuries put forward. Rational government is this, so to speak: given the nature of the state, it can hold down its enemies for an indeterminate length of time. It can do so only if it increases its own strength. And its enemies do likewise. The state whose only concern would be to hold out would most certainly come to disaster. This idea is a very important one. It is bound up with a new historical outlook; indeed, it implies that states are realities that must hold out for an indefinite length of historical time—and in a disputed geographical area.

4. Finally, we can see that reason of state, understood as rational government able to increase the state's strength in accordance with itself, presupposes the constitution of a certain type of knowledge. Government is only possible if the strength of the state is known; it can thus be sustained. The state's capacity, and the means to enlarge it, must be known. The strength and capacities

of the other states must also be known. Indeed, the governed state must hold out against the others. Government therefore entails more than just implementing general principles of reason, wisdom, and prudence. Knowledge is necessary—concrete, precise, and measured knowledge as to the state's strength. The art of governing, characteristic of reason of state, is intimately bound up with the development of what was then called either political "statistics" or "arithmetic," that is, the knowledge of different states' respective forces. Such knowledge was indispensable for correct government.

Briefly speaking, then: reason of state is not an art of government according to divine, natural, or human laws. It doesn't have to respect the general order of the world. It's government in accordance with the state's strength. It's government whose aim is to increase this strength within an extensive and competitive framework.

So what the seventeenth- and eighteenth-century authors understand by "the police" is very different from what we put under the term. It would be worth studying why these authors are mostly Italians and Germans, but whatever! What they understand by "police" is not an institution or mechanism functioning within the state but a governmental technology peculiar to the state—domains, techniques, targets where the state intervenes.

To be clear and simple, I will exemplify what I'm saying with a text that is both utopian and a project. It's one of the first utopia programs for a policed state. Louis Turquet de Mayerne drew it up and presented it in 1611 to the Dutch States General. In his book *Science and Rationalism in the Government of Louis XIV,* J. King draws attention to the importance of this strange work. Its title is *Aristo-democratic Monarchy.* That's enough to show what is important in the author's eyes—not so much choosing between these different types of constitution as their mixture in view to a vital end, namely, the state. Turquet also calls it the City, the Republic, or yet again, the Police.

Here is the organization Turquet proposes. Four grand officials rank beside the king. One is in charge of justice; another, of the army; the third, of the exchequer, that is, the king's taxes and revenues; the fourth is in charge of the *police.* It seems that this officer's role was to have been mainly a moral one. According to Turquet, he was to foster among the people "modesty, charity, loyalty, industriousness, friendly cooperation, honesty." We recognize the traditional idea that the subject's virtue ensures the kingdom's good management. But, when we come down to the details, the outlook is somewhat different.

Turquet suggests that in each province, there should be boards keeping law and order. There should be two that see to people; the other two see to things. The first board pertaining to people was to see to the positive, active, productive aspects of life. In other words, it was concerned with education; determining each one's tastes and aptitudes; the choosing of occupations—useful ones (each person over the age of twenty-five had to be enrolled on a register noting his occupation). Those not usefully employed were regarded as the dregs of society.

The second board was to see to the negative aspects of life:

the poor (widows, orphans, the aged) requiring help; the unem-
ployed; those whose activities required financial aid (no interest was to be charged); public health (disease, epidemics); and
accidents such as fire and flood.

One of the boards concerned with things was to specialize
in commodities and manufactured goods. It was to indicate
what was to be produced and how; it was also to control mar-
kets and trading. The fourth board would see to the "demesne,"
that is, the territory, space: private property, legacies, dona-
tions, sales were to be controlled; manorial rights were to be
reformed; roads, rivers, public buildings, and forests would also
be seen to.

In many features, the text is akin to the political utopias
that were so numerous at the time. But it is also contemporary
with the great theoretical discussions on reason of state and
the administrative organization of monarchies. It is highly rep-
resentative of what the epoch considered a traditionally governed state's tasks to be.

What does this text demonstrate?

1. The "police" appears as an administration heading the
   state, together with the judiciary, the army, and the exchequer. True. Yet in fact, it embraces everything else.
   Turquet says so: "It branches out into all of the people's
   conditions, everything they do or undertake. Its field
   comprises justice, finance, and the army."

2. The *police* includes everything. But from an extremely
   particular point of view. Men and things are envisioned
   as to their relationships: men's coexistence on a terri-

tory; their relationships as to property; what they produce; what is exchanged on the market. It also considers how they live, the diseases and accidents that can befall them. What the police sees to is a live, active, productive man. Turquet employs a remarkable expression: "The police's true object is man."

3. Such intervention in men's activities could well be qualified as totalitarian. What are the aims pursued? They fall into two categories. First, the police has to do with everything providing the city with adornment, form, and splendor. *Splendor* denotes not only the beauty of a state ordered to perfection but also its strength, its vigor. The police therefore ensures and highlights the state's vigor. Second, the police's other purpose is to foster working and trading relations between men, as well as aid and mutual help. There again, the word Turquet uses is important: the police must ensure "communication" among men, in the broad sense of the word—otherwise, men wouldn't be able to live, or their lives would be precarious, poverty-stricken, and perpetually threatened.

And here, we can make out what is, I think, an important idea. As a form of rational intervention wielding political power over men, the role of the police is to supply them with a little extra life—and, by so doing, supply the state with a little extra strength. This is done by controlling "communication," that is, the common activities of individuals (work, production, exchange, accommodation).

You'll object: "But that's only the utopia of some obscure author. You can hardly deduce any significant consequences from it!" But *I* say: Turquet's book is but one example of a huge literature circulating in most European countries of the day. The fact that it is over-simple and yet very detailed brings out all the better the characteristics that could be recognized elsewhere. Above all, I'd say that such ideas were not stillborn. They spread all through the seventeenth and eighteenth centuries, either as applied policies (such as Cameralism or mercantilism), or as subjects to be taught (the German *Polizeiwissenschaft*; let us not forget that this was the title under which the science of administration was taught in Germany).

These are the two perspectives that I'd like, not to study, but at least to suggest. First I'll refer to a French administrative compendium, then to a German textbook.

1. Every historian knows N. De Lamare's compendium, *Treaty on the Police*. At the beginning of the eighteenth century, this administrator undertook the compilation of the whole kingdom's police regulations. It's an infinite source of very valuable information. The general conception of the police that such a quantity of rules and regulations could convey to an administrator like De Lamare is what I'd like to emphasize.

   De Lamare says that the police must see to eleven things within the state: (1) religion; (2) morals; (3) health; (4) supplies; (5) roads, highways, town buildings; (6) public safety; (7) the liberal arts (roughly speaking, arts and science); (8) trade; (9) factories; (10) manservants and laborers; (11) the poor.

The same classification features in every treatise concerning the police. As in Turquet's utopia program, apart from the army, justice properly speaking, and direct taxes, the police apparently sees to everything. The same thing can be said differently: royal power had asserted itself against feudalism, thanks to the support of an armed force and by developing a judicial system and establishing a tax system. These were the ways in which royal power was traditionally wielded. Now, "the police" is the term covering the whole new field in which centralized political and administrative power can intervene.

Now, what is the logic behind intervention in cultural rites, small-scale production techniques, intellectual life, and the road network?

De Lamare's answer seems a bit hesitant. Here he says, "The police sees to everything pertaining to men's *happiness*"; there he says, "The police sees to everything regulating *'society'* (social relations) carried on between men"; elsewhere he says that the police sees to *living*. This is the definition I will dwell upon. It's the most original and it clarifies the other two, and De Lamare himself dwells upon it. He makes the following remarks as to the police's eleven objects. The police deals with religion, not, of course, from the viewpoint of dogmatic truth but from that of the moral quality of life. In seeing to health and supplies, it deals with the preservation of life; concerning trade, factories, workers, the poor, and public order—it deals with the conveniences of life. In seeing to the theater, literature, entertainment, its object is life's pleasures. In short, life is the object of the police: the indispensable, the useful, and the superfluous. That people survive, live, and even do better than just that: this is what the police has to ensure.

And so we link up with the other definitions De Lamare proposes: "The sole purpose of the police is to lead man to the utmost happiness to be enjoyed in this life." Or, again, the police cares for the good of the soul (thanks to religion and morality), the good of the body (food, health, clothing, housing), wealth (industry, trade, labor). Or, again, the police sees to the benefits that can be derived only from living in society.

2. Now let us have a look at the German textbooks. They were used to teach the science of administration somewhat later on. It was taught in various universities, especially in Göttingen, and was extremely important for continental Europe. Here it was that the Prussian, Austrian, and Russian civil servants—those who were to carry out Joseph II's and Catherine the Great's reforms—were trained. Certain Frenchmen, especially in Napoleon's entourage, knew the teachings of *Polizeiwissenschaft* very well.

What was to be found in these textbooks?

Huhenthal's *Liber de politia* featured the following items: the number of citizens; religion and morals; health; food; the safety of persons and of goods (particularly in reference to fires and floods); the administration of justice; citizens' conveniences and pleasures (how to obtain them, how to restrict them). Then comes a series of chapters about rivers, forests, mines, brine pits, housing, and, finally, several chapters on how to acquire goods either through farming, industry, or trade.

In his *Précis for the Police,* J. P. Willebrand speaks successively of morals, trades and crafts, health, safety, and last of all, town building and planning. Considering the subjects at least, there isn't a great deal of difference from De Lamare's.

But the most important of these texts is Johann Heinrich Gottlob von Justi's *Elements of Police.* The police's specific purpose is still defined as live individuals living in society. Nevertheless, the way von Justi organizes his book is somewhat different. He studies first what he calls the "state's landed property," that is, its territory. He considers it in two different aspects: how it is inhabited (town versus country), and then who inhabit these territories (the number of people, their growth, health, mortality, immigration). Von Justi then analyzes the "goods and chattels," that is, the commodities, manufactured goods, and their circulation, which involve problems pertaining to cost, credit, and currency. Finally, the last part is devoted to the conduct of individuals: their morals their occupational capabilities, their honesty, and how they respect the law.

In my opinion, von Justi's work is a much more advanced demonstration of how the police problem evolved than De Lamare's introduction to his compendium of statutes. There are four reasons for this.

First, von Justi defines much more clearly what the

central paradox of *police* is. The police, he says, is what enables the state to increase its power and exert its strength to the full. On the other hand, the police has to keep the citizens happy—happiness being understood as survival, life, and improved living. He perfectly defines what I feel to be the aim of the modern art of government, or state rationality, namely, to develop those elements constitutive of individuals' lives in such a way that their development also fosters the strength of the state.

Von Justi then draws a distinction between this task, which he calls *Polizei*, as do his contemporaries, and *Politik, die Politik. Die Politik* is basically a negative task: it consists in the state's fighting against its internal and external enemies. *Polizei*, however, is a positive task: it has to foster both citizens' lives *and* the state's strength.

And here is the important point: von Justi insists much more than does De Lamare on a notion that became increasingly important during the eighteenth century—population. Population was understood as a group of live individuals. Their characteristics were those of all the individuals belonging to the same species, living side by side. (Thus, they presented mortality and fecundity rates; they were subject to epidemics, overpopulation; they presented a certain type of territorial distribution.) True, De Lamare did use the term "life" to characterize the concern of the police, but the emphasis he gave it wasn't very pronounced. Proceeding through the eighteenth century, and especially in Germany, we see that what is defined as the object of the police is population, that is, a group of beings living in a given area.

And last, one only has to read von Justi to see that it is not only a utopia, as with Turquet, or a compendium of systematically filed regulations. Von Justi claims to draw up a *Polizeiwissenschaft*. His book isn't simply a list of prescriptions: it's also a grid through which the state—that is, territory, resources, population, towns, and so on—can be observed. Von Justi combines "statistics" (the description of states) with the art of government. *Polizeiwissenschaft* is at once an art of government and a method for the analysis of a population living on a territory.

Such historical considerations must appear to be very remote; they must seem useless in regard to present-day concerns. I wouldn't go as far as Hermann Hesse, who says that only the "constant reference to history, the past, and antiquity" is fecund. But experience has taught me that the history of various forms of rationality is sometimes more effective in unsettling our certitudes and dogmatism than is abstract criticism. For centuries, religion couldn't bear having its history told. Today, our schools of rationality balk at having their history written, which is no doubt significant.

What I've wanted to show is a direction for research. These are only the rudiments of something I've been working at for the last two years. It's the historical analysis of what we could call, using an obsolete term, the "art of government."

This study rests upon several basic assumptions. I'd sum them up like this:

1. Power is not a substance. Neither is it a mysterious property whose origin must be delved into. Power is only a certain type of relation between individuals. Such relations are specific, that is, they have nothing to do with exchange, production, communication, even though they combine with them. The characteristic feature of power is that some men can more or less entirely determine other men's conduct—but never exhaustively or coercively. A man who is chained up and beaten is subject to force being exerted over him, not power. But if he can be induced to speak, when his ultimate recourse could have been to hold his tongue, preferring death, then he has been caused to behave in a certain way. His freedom has been subjected to power. He has been submitted to government. If an individual can remain free, however little his freedom may be, power can subject him to government. There is no power without potential refusal or revolt.

2. As for all relations among men, many factors determine power. Yet rationalization is also constantly working away at it. There are specific forms to such rationalization. It differs from the rationalization peculiar to economic processes, or to production and communication techniques; it differs from that of scientific discourse. The government of men by men—whether they form small or large groups, whether it is power

exerted by men over women, or by adults over children, or by one class over another, or by a bureaucracy over a population—involves a certain type of rationality. It doesn't involve instrumental violence.

3. Consequently, those who resist or rebel against a form of power cannot merely be content to denounce violence or criticize an institution. Nor is it enough to cast the blame on reason in general. What has to be questioned is the form of rationality at stake. The criticism of power wielded over the mentally sick or mad cannot be restricted to psychiatric institutions; nor can those questioning the power to punish be content with denouncing prisons as total institutions. The question is: How are such relations of power rationalized? Asking it is the only way to avoid other institutions, with the same objectives and the same effects, from taking their stead.

4. For several centuries, the state has been one of the most remarkable, one of the most redoubtable, forms of human government.

Very significantly, political criticism has reproached the state with being simultaneously a factor for individualization and a totalitarian principle. Just to look at nascent state rationality, just to see what its first policing project was, makes it clear that, right from the start, the state is both individualizing and totalitarian. Opposing the individual and his interests to it is just as hazardous as opposing it with the community and its requirements.

Political rationality has grown and imposed itself all

throughout the history of Western societies. It first took its stand on the idea of pastoral power, then on that of reason of state. Its inevitable effects are both individualization and totalization. Liberation can come only from attacking not just one of these two effects but political rationality's very roots.

6.

Confronting Governments: Human Rights[1]

Michel Foucault

We are just private individuals here, with no other grounds for speaking, or for speaking together, than a certain shared difficulty in enduring what is taking place.

Of course, we accept the obvious fact that there's not much that we can do about the reasons why some men and women would rather leave their country than live in it. The fact is beyond our reach.

Who appointed us, then? No one. And that is precisely what constitutes our right. It seems to me that we need to bear in mind three principles that, I believe, guide this initiative, and many others that have preceded it: the *Île-de-Lumière*, Cape Anamour, the Airplane for El Salvador, Terre des Hommes, Amnesty International.

1. There exists an international citizenship that has its rights and its duties, and that obliges one to speak out

against every abuse of power, whoever its author, whoever its victims. After all, we are all members of the community of the governed, and thereby obliged to show mutual solidarity.

2. Because they claim to be concerned with the welfare of societies, governments arrogate to themselves the right to pass off as profit or loss the human unhappiness that their decisions provoke or their negligence permits. It is a duty of this international citizenship to always bring the testimony of people's suffering to the eyes and ears of governments, sufferings for which it's untrue that they are not responsible. The suffering of men must never be a silent residue of policy. It grounds an absolute right to stand up and speak to those who hold power.

3. We must reject the division of labor so often proposed to us: individuals can get indignant and talk; governments will reflect and act. It's true that good governments appreciate the holy indignation of the governed, provided it remains lyrical. I think we need to be aware that very often it is those who govern who talk, are capable only of talking, and want only to talk. Experience shows that one can and must refuse the theatrical role of pure and simple indignation that is proposed to us. Amnesty International, Terre des Hommes, and Médecins du monde are initiatives that have created this new right—that of private individuals to effectively intervene in the sphere of international policy and strategy. The will of individuals must make a place for itself

in a reality of which governments have attempted to reserve a monopoly for themselves, that monopoly which we need to wrest from them little by little and day by day.

Notes

1. The occasion for this statement, published in *Libération* in June 1984, was the announcement in Geneva of the creation of an International Committee against Piracy.